Becoming Hungarian

a memoir

Erika Reich Giles

Content in Chapters One through Four is drawn from the essay "Flight from Hungary," originally published in *Crab Orchard Review*. Chapter Five was published in slightly different form in *Clackamas Literary Review* and an anthology, *Siblings and Autism*, Jessica Kingsley Publishers, 2011. Chapter Six originated as an essay published in *North Dakota Quarterly* and Chapter Thirteen as an essay in *Under the Sun*.

Publisher's Cataloging-in-Publication Data
Names: Giles, Erika Reich, author.
Title: Becoming Hungarian : a memoir / Erika Reich Giles.
Description: Portland, Oregon : Montiron Press, [2024]
Identifiers: ISBN: 979-8-218-33697-4 | LCCN: 2024905955
Subjects: LCSH: Giles, Erika Reich. | Hungarian Americans--Biography. | Political refugees--United States--Biography. | Refugee children--United States--Biography. | Communism--Hungary. | Confiscations--Hungary--1945-1989. | Hungary--Politics and government--1945-1989. | Hungary--Social conditions--1945-1989.
Classification: LCC: E184.H95 G55 2024 | DDC: 973/.0494511/0092--dc23

BIOGRAPHY & AUTOBIOGRAPHY / Personal Memoirs

Cover and book design by Rachel Valliere, Printed Page Studios
Back photograph by Meghan Paddock Farrell Photography

This memoir represents actual events in the life of the author as truthfully as recollection permits and/or can be verified by research. Others present at those events may remember them differently.

Printed in the United States of America.

Montiron Press
Portland, Oregon

For my parents

Contents

Prologue

Billings, Montana. March 15, 1959. The ten or so Hungarian refugee families in this remote, arid town on the western edge of the Great Plains are celebrating Hungarian Independence Day. A major holiday in their homeland, March 15 commemorates the freedom fighters of the failed 1848 Revolution against Austria. The adults in the group still miss Hungary, five thousand miles away and locked behind the Iron Curtain for the past ten years, except for a brief period of freedom during the failed 1956 Revolution against the Soviets. Some in the room escaped then, following in the footsteps of others who'd fled during the Communist takeover after World War II. They planned this gathering to alleviate their homesickness for a country they may never see again, and centered it on their hopes for the future, their children.

I am one of those children. Ten years old, all elbows and knees, my ash blonde hair curled into ringlets and my lips reddened with a touch of lipstick, I wear a splendid traditional costume my mother sewed for me. The dress is white organdy, with puffed sleeves and a full skirt trimmed with narrow bands of red, white, and green, the colors of the Hungarian flag. Over it, I wear a lace apron trimmed in the same colors and a red velvet vest decorated with loops of gold braid. On my head is a matching *párta*, a coronet with two wide sashes of red, white, and green satin ribbon tied in a bow at my crown and flowing past my waist.

A dozen of us—mostly girls, ranging in age from six to late teens, several wearing costumes like mine—stand in front of our parents in the community room of the local YWCA. The program begins with everyone singing "The Star-Spangled Banner" in a chorus ranging from booming basses to squeaky sopranos, accompanied by my older sister, Judy, on the piano. A tribute to our adopted country, on whose shores my family arrived seven years ago, in 1952. Next, we sing "Himnusz," Hungary's national anthem, which implores God to bless the Hungarian people and protect them from the enemies who have threatened them through a history dating to the late ninth century, when the military leader Árpád led the Magyars westward from Asia to the area of Europe's Carpathian Basin that is now Hungary.

Individual performances follow. I fidget in my seat watching those who precede me, including Gábor, a gangling teenager reciting an epic poem with forceful inflections, and my pale, dark-eyed cousin, Suzie, my age, singing a folk song in soft, breathy tones. She and her parents, my mother's sister Aunt Évi and Uncle Laci, and our maternal grandparents, Nagymama and Nagypapa, joined us in Billings after the 1956 uprising.

Finally, Mrs. Jakab, the emcee, an imposing woman with salt-and-pepper hair, announces that "Reich Erika" (in Hungarian, the surname is stated first) will recite a poem, "Magyar Vagyok" ("I'm Hungarian") by Pohárnok Jenő. My mother, the prompter, elegant in a black skirt and white blouse, gives me an encouraging smile from the sidelines as I take my place behind the microphone. My legs tremble slightly. I repeat the poem's title and author in a high, clear voice and begin. I recite the author's sentiments: his love for his adopted country tempered by a resolve never to forget Hungary; his coping with physical distance by keeping his home close in thought; his certainty that, as long as he lives, he'll never be anything but Hungarian.

I had memorized the seven lines of the poem in the preceding weeks by reciting the words over and over, to myself walking to and from school, to my parents sitting on our living room sofa, to Nagymama at her kitchen table. But I had no idea what they meant. I didn't remember Hungary. I didn't remember the first two months of my life there. I didn't remember my mother carrying me in her arms as she escaped across the border toward freedom.

PART I

Looking Back

chapter one

Inquiry

I TORE OPEN the envelope to find a rare letter from my ninety-one-year-old father. Dated April 15, 2003, it was a page and a half long, typed single-spaced on thin, slightly discolored white paper. "Dear Erika," he began, "I give you the story of our flight from Communist Hungary."

A lump formed in my throat as I imagined him sitting in his easy chair—white-haired, long legs bent awkwardly at arthritic knees, blue eyes squinting behind silver-framed glasses at the Hermès Baby typewriter in his lap—painstakingly searching with his index finger for each key to commit the ache of those long-ago memories to paper. Reading his words, I realized he was mostly reiterating the bare facts I already knew. Still, by the time I reached his closing, "With best wishes and with all my love," and "Dad" signed in his bold, slanted hand, I was filled with gratitude for the efforts of a father with whom I'd always shared a special bond. At the same time, I hungered for more of the story: characters, scenes, descriptions.

My father was responding to a request I had made of my parents during a visit to Billings a year and a half earlier, in the wake of 9/11. Jolted by the tragic reminder that time is fleeting and that opportunities can easily be missed, I had asked my parents to record their memories of the events surrounding my birth in Hungary in 1948 that forever changed our lives. This letter was one of only a handful I had ever received from my father. Despite our closeness, he preferred to leave the family correspondence to my mother.

For most of my life, I had known only the story's outlines, illustrated with hazy images of my paternal grandfather Opapa's overcoat, a bicycle, a bus. "Átok Kommunisták" (Damned Communists), my parents railed during my childhood when discussing the upheaval that began in Szombathely, our hometown of forty thousand people ten miles from the Austrian border. Small wonder. The Communists who took over the country after World War II with the help of the Soviets reversed their fortunes, setting them on a challenging course that culminated thousands of miles away in Montana. But my parents volunteered few specifics, no doubt reluctant to tear the bandage from a wound never completely healed. I inhaled their silence, wrapped it around me. With that silence, I tried to deny to the world outside our small Hungarian enclave that I was born in Hungary, that we came to the United States as refugees, that we spoke Hungarian at home, that we were different. My father's wistful references to the former Reich Gépgyár, his family's agricultural machine factory, "Amikor mienk volt a gyár …" (When we owned the factory …), manifested a regret that clung to my parents and tugged them toward the past. I had no use for the past. I wanted to be like everyone else. American. Only as an adult living far from home did I fully succeed in that endeavor. But in middle age, the flickering flame of difference at my core, fanned by my father's letter, scorched my resistance to the past, driving me to sift through my family's history, to reclaim my heritage.

I questioned my father. I questioned my mother. Countless phone calls. Several visits from my home on Mercer Island, a Seattle suburb in the middle of Lake Washington, to Billings. It was more contact than we'd had since I left home for college nearly four decades earlier.

"What was Opapa like?" I asked my father during one of our early phone conversations, referring to my paternal grandfather. I sat in my bookshelf-lined study over the garage of our rambler, looking out over the rooftops at Seattle's verdant hills in the distance. My fingers were poised over the keys of my laptop to record his response.

"Nem értem" (I don't understand), he said, his voice vigorous despite his age.

"Are you wearing your hearing aids?" I asked, raising my voice. His hearing loss, which had gradually increased over the years, was profound.

"Yes, but I don't think they're on." A pause as he fumbled with the instruments. "Okay, now what were you asking?"

"Opapa, what was he like?" I asked again, louder yet, this time in Hungarian. It was easier to formulate my questions in English, but he understood me better when I spoke our native language.

"A kind man. Reserved. He cared about his employees," he said.

"Did you get along with him?" I'd heard that he hadn't, that he had chafed under my Opapa's authority.

"Of course," he said.

"You never disagreed?"

"No," he said with a note of finality. I decided not to push him. Still, I wondered whether my grandfather's employees and people in the community had viewed him as my father described him.

"Who smuggled us to Austria?" I asked.

"An army sergeant," he answered. All he remembered about the man was that he had been near his own age, in his thirties. I was curious about his name, what he looked like.

"How did you meet him?"

"What?" he asked.

I repeated the question in Hungarian, louder.

And so it went. Hour-long phone calls that exhausted us both. My father had suggested that I write down my questions, enabling him to answer them in writing, but I wanted to be able to clarify his answers, to ask follow-up questions. And I welcomed the excuse to talk with him. He was laconic by nature, and keeping a conversation going with him could be difficult. But my project sparked his enthusiasm and inspired him to talk far more than he usually did. Even so, he focused mostly on the big picture and remembered few of the details I craved.

Our calls were so laborious that I ended up gathering the most complete information when I was home in Billings, with my eighty-year-old mother interjecting comments as my father and I talked. I stayed with them in their 1920s bungalow on a shady street near Pioneer Park and downtown, where we had moved when I was in sixth grade. The scent of garlic mingled with sweet Hungarian paprika that I remembered from childhood filled the house as she stood at the stove in the compact kitchen, stirring cubes of beef sizzling in oil for goulash, her hands gnarled by rheumatoid arthritis. "I'm not sure it's good to remember these things," she told me, a troubled look creasing her remarkably smooth face.

I sat in the living room on the beige velour sofa across from my father in his roll-armed chair in the corner. His head was bent over a crossword puzzle, and I hesitated to interrupt him. Instead, I absorbed the atmosphere of the familiar space, separated from the dining room by a pair of five-foot-tall built-in bookcases filled with framed family photographs and novels and nonfiction books in English, German, and Hungarian. These rooms with their mahogany furniture and burgundy oriental rugs and sheer-curtained windows had been the scene of many family celebrations and parties with our Hungarian friends. They had also witnessed my adolescent clashes with my mother over boys and curfews and my forays into smoking and drinking. My father worked nights then and was often absent when I misbehaved. Those confrontations exacerbated a mother-daughter relationship that, though loving, simmered with tension beneath the surface.

I studied a pair of oil portraits of Gypsy women over the fireplace, the centerpiece of artwork that also included gold-framed black-and-white photographs of Hungarian street scenes and watercolor landscapes. Ceramic vases and figurines and boxes decorated with Hungarian floral patterns sat on side tables. On the coffee table in front of me, albums and books and a silver tray with greeting cards vied for space with piles of magazines: *Harper's*, *Smithsonian*, *Newsweek*.

My father looked up and gazed at me fondly. "What was Omama and Opapa's house like?" I asked him, my mind still on home decor. He had returned to live in his childhood home after college and my mother joined him there when they were married, less than a year before my birth and our escape.

"It was big, and there was a courtyard," he began.

"They had a grand piano and Persian rugs and furniture upholstered in velvet," my mother called from the dining room. "We ate our meals with your grandparents at a large mahogany dining room table," she added before launching into more details about life in the household. The more she told me, the more I longed to know—about the individual rooms and what had happened in them, about the view from each window, about the surrounding neighborhood. My mother proved to be a wellspring of facts about how people looked and acted, and where and when events occurred.

I also questioned my sister, Judy, five years older. Our relationship was still strained at times by remnants of childhood resentments, but we had grown closer as adults. We phoned and emailed and visited several times a year, either at my home or hers in Portland, Oregon.

"What do you remember about escaping from Hungary?" I asked her during a visit.

She was silent for a moment, a pensive look in eyes expertly made up with smoky eyeshadow, eyeliner, and mascara. "I wore my favorite dress. It was yellow with white daisies on it," she said.

"Anything else?"

"When the folks took me to Vasvár to say goodbye to her family, Nagymama and Nagypapa wouldn't stop sobbing." She paused. "That's about all I remember." Her tone was matter-of-fact about a scene that must have been wrenching. But unlike me, Judy doesn't dwell on emotions, and I knew better than to push her. She was only five years old at the time and may not have grasped the magnitude of what was happening. The details she did remember were from the months and years after we left Hungary, facts I would gather much later.

Even my parents' more extensive recollections were fragmented, incomplete, sometimes contradictory. "Were you warned of the factory takeover?" I asked them at one point, referring to the 250-employee agricultural machine factory my grandfather had founded in our hometown. My father said yes, my mother said no. Only after talking further did they finally agree that there had been no *overt* warning. The story emerged over many months, haphazardly, in disconnected pieces. From them, I began to create a chronology, plugging incidents into the right spots as I gained more clarity about them.

How did I visualize the memories I gathered? Black-and-white photographs from that era on my parents' bedroom wall. The two of them, attractive, smiling, her blonde head inclined toward his dark-haired one. My dark-suited Opapa in one of the few images our family had of him, with close-cropped white hair, his narrow face serious, his round eyes staring into the distance. My Omama, with wavy hair close to her prominent cheekbones, enveloped in a fur coat. Color snapshots of the family house and factory taken by a family friend in the 1980s. A pocket map of Szombathely and the surrounding area marked by my mother with the location of the house and factory and the escape route. Her book of old postcards of the city and its landmarks: the main square, the train station, the Lutheran church where I was baptized. My mother's diagram of the floor plan of the house; my father's diagrams of the layouts of the factory's two locations, Plants

A and B. *A History of Modern Hungary: 1868–1986,* by Jörg Hoensch, and other books and documents about Hungarian history. And when all else failed, I tapped my own imagination to fill in the blanks.

Characters emerged. My parents as a joyful young married couple with high hopes for the future. Opapa as an astute businessman who also cared about his employees. Omama as a dignified matron with a rebellious streak not unlike that of her granddaughter. My family's story was coming to life.

chapter two

Cataclysm

My parents, Sándor and Vilmy Reich, had been married less than a year on March 26, 1948, the day their lives began to unravel. My mother was eight months pregnant with me. They were living with my father's parents in their stately, tile-roofed stucco row house on a street lined with locust trees near the west edge of Szombathely. My father was Opapa's deputy at the Reich Gépgyár, the factory my grandfather had established thirty years earlier, where he was the chief executive. My mother had been working for several years as the factory's payroll clerk.

The miseries of World War II, culminating with heavy bombing by the Allies that reduced buildings in the town center to rubble and left hundreds dead, were behind them. Like most people in town, my parents were only vaguely aware of the threat that began at the end of the war: the slow, insidious takeover of Hungary by the Communists, backed by the Soviets who occupied the country after driving out the Nazis. The Communists were infiltrating the government, the political parties, the labor unions. They were confiscating land and businesses. But Szombathely was more than a hundred miles from Budapest, the capital, and by then the

Communists also controlled the press. No doubt they stifled news of their activities, to keep the citizens off-balance, to retain the crucial element of surprise.

That day's beginning was lost to my parents, perhaps because it was so ordinary, with nothing to distinguish it from any other day that began with breakfast in my grandparents' dining room. Still, I feel compelled to imagine them there, to use details I know to create a sense of how the cataclysmic can collide with the commonplace, with no warning, no chance to prepare.

My parents sit with Omama and Opapa at a table covered in ivory damask, eating with silver utensils from china plates. A young female servant stands by the doorway, waiting to do my grandmother's bidding. Beyond the lace-curtained windows, the factory buildings adjacent to the house awaken with workers' shouts and greetings and the buzz of machines starting up.

"Hogy érzed magadat?" (How do you feel?) my father asks my mother, reaching across the table and wrapping his long fingers around her small hand. He still marvels at his good fortune in marrying this lovely twenty-four-year-old woman with blonde hair cascading down her back. Approaching his midthirties, he had begun to wonder whether he would ever find a suitable wife.

"Egy kicsit fáradt vagyok" (I'm a little tired), she answers with a wan smile, pushing away her plate of half-finished scrambled eggs. She loves her handsome husband, so solicitous of her welfare. But she still feels ill at ease in this staid household, a stark contrast to her parents' home, where people laugh and shout and interrupt each other. She's uncertain how to act with her employer, now that he's also her father-in-law, or her mother-in-law, who sometimes studies her with heavy-lidded eyes when she thinks my mother isn't looking. She knows it's all part of the price of marrying the son of her boss, but she longs for the day that the house her father-in-law has promised them will be built, so she and her husband can embark on their own life together.

"I may go shopping for baby clothes while you're at work," Omama says in her low voice. My mother flashes her a smile of gratitude. How can she question the kindness of her in-laws when they have done everything possible to welcome her, to make her feel at home? She resolves to put rebellious thoughts out of her mind.

"Don't forget the management meeting Ihász has called for this afternoon," Opapa tells my father. He is referring to the factory's shop steward, a mediocre employee whose loyalties are questionable. He shifts his lanky body in his chair. "Maybe he has another idea to improve working conditions."

"Or it might be an employee grievance," my father says. His angular features show no sign of worry.

"I hope it doesn't take too long," Opapa says. He cares about his employees. During the war, he bought firewood and distributed it to them so they could heat their homes in winter. And afterward, when rampant inflation rendered the pengő worthless, customers could only pay him in goods like cabbages, potatoes, and sacks of flour. He passed those on to his employees to keep them from starving. But as a mechanical engineer, he's always been more excited about repairing the factory's machines and modifying them to make new products than dealing with personnel problems.

My father looks at his watch. "We should leave," he says. He goes to the other side of the table and pulls out my mother's chair. She heaves herself out of her seat. Her belly is becoming uncomfortably large, and she hopes she will deliver soon. Still, she's glad she decided to remain at work as long as possible. At the factory, her duties are familiar, her role well-defined. She strolls arm in arm with my father behind Opapa from the dining room to the kitchen and down the stairs to the factory beyond.

How did two opposites like Sándor and Vilmy end up together? The elder of two children, the only son of a prominent Szombathely family, my father had grown up amid wealth and privilege. With his sister, Marianne, he was in line to inherit the factory where he had worked for sixteen years since becoming a mechanical engineer like his father. My mother was the elder of two daughters of a Russian-immigrant gardener and a legal secretary of modest means in Vasvár, a village twelve miles away. He was reserved, polite, a perfectionist. She was outspoken, passionate, volatile. He was Lutheran; she had been raised Catholic. He was a bachelor. She had been married previously, to a soldier in the Hungarian Army who had fought in the war. She was also the mother of a five-year-old daughter named Judy, who was often absent from the household, visiting the maternal grandparents who had cared for her while her mother worked at the factory. Perhaps it was precisely those differences that had attracted my parents to each other. My father might have sought excitement and stimulation, a balance to a family in which emotions were held firmly in check. My mother might have longed for calm and stability after a failed marriage. Perhaps it was also a case of physical attraction—of two pairs of blue eyes studying each other as he leaned over her desk to ask a question, as they brushed past each other in a hallway—between a mustached man with dark hair combed sideways over a high, intelligent forehead and a petite, shapely woman with a dusting of freckles on her nose.

* * *

That afternoon, two men stood on the stage in the factory's meeting hall, twenty-five or thirty managers and supervisors crowded into chairs before them. Ihász, the slight and unprepossessing shop steward, called the meeting to order. But it was his companion, a burly, gray-haired stranger named Ligeti, eyes set too wide in a face my father recalled as frog-like and distasteful, who was in charge. He represented the Communist Party.

Ligeti began with a proclamation: "Eddig mienk volt a tűdő baj, a szegénység; de mostantól kezdbe, tieteké a gyár és magatoknak dolgoztok." (Until now, tuberculosis and poverty have been our lot, but from now on, this factory is yours and you are working for yourselves.) Half a century later, my father recited the words to me without hesitation. He even imitated Ligeti's delivery, his voice growing higher and more frenzied with each syllable. I imagined the man jabbing his fist toward the audience in emphasis, his broad face sweaty, flushed.

My sixty-eight-year-old grandfather listened impassively from the front row. A serious man, reserved. Perhaps he was reflecting on the major achievement of his engineering career: building a two-person machine repair shop into this 250-employee manufacturer of brick press and steam engine components, sifting machines, beet shredders, wine presses, wheat cutters, and water turbines. He had established the factory's original site by purchasing existing structures and building new ones behind the family home. Seven one- and two-story stucco buildings with tile roofs housing offices, a foundry, and machine, locksmith, and cabinet shops eventually surrounded a dirt courtyard that had replaced a backyard of plum trees and a vegetable garden. Later, he bought from the estate of his former employer a failing iron foundry and related shops two blocks away, creating the factory's second location, Plant B.

My father, as reticent as Opapa, also revealed no emotion. Yet the impact of the factory on his life had been, if anything, even greater than on his father's. His childhood had been steeped in the factory, in the buildings, the craftsmen operating the lathes and drill presses within them, the whir and clack and whine of the machines. He spent all his free time in the shops, watching Törökös grinding machine parts or Szabados casting them from molten iron. He asked questions, contemplated the answers. He apprenticed in the factory after finishing high school, rotating through the iron foundry and various shops before beginning his mechanical engineering studies at the Ingenieurschule Weimar in Germany. After his graduation, he returned to work alongside Opapa, starting as a draftsman and working his way up to overseeing a hundred employees in Plant B's iron foundry. And the factory had led him to my mother—to love and marriage and a baby on the way.

The moments after Ligeti's announcement were a blur in my father's mind. But he remembered the mortal blow, like a hammer smashing a vase of fine Herend porcelain, that Ligeti then delivered to Opapa: "You are on permanent leave, starting today." My grandfather was to leave the premises immediately after the meeting. He was to stop nowhere on his way out—not in the shops, not in his office, not in the courtyard. He was to take nothing with him, not even his coat.

The factory employees were silent at Ligeti's words. No doubt some, like Ihász, who became the new manager, were elated. Still, they refrained from gloating. Others might have been shocked, or they feared antagonizing such ruthless men. At the end of the meeting, Ihász invited the audience to stand and sing "L'Internacionale," the Communist anthem. The group sang of workers arising, of abandoning tradition, of revolt. Opapa and my father stood rigid, stone-faced, silent.

My father recounted what had happened during one of our many phone calls, and I paused to absorb his account of Opapa's public humiliation at the hands of the Communists. "Are you sure about the coat?" I finally asked. From childhood, I remembered hearing, "All they let him take was his coat." But perhaps it had only been my child's mind, demanding fairness, that had returned my grandfather's coat to him.

"Yes," my father replied. "Opapa walked out of the factory with nothing."

I was stunned. The overcoat, perhaps of black cashmere, a coat befitting the largest employer in Szombathely, had been the final vestige of all my family lost that day. Was anything left?

My parents forgot what happened afterward. But my linear view of the world doesn't permit me to leave the end of the meeting dangling, with no attempt at resolution. With bits and pieces gleaned from my parents' memories, I imagine what might have happened next.

Opapa turns to my father. "Go back to work like nothing happened," he murmurs. "Don't let them intimidate you." He then leaves quickly, head down, speaking to no one else. Outside, he crosses the courtyard to the street. He buttons his suit jacket against the March breeze and thrusts his hands in his pockets. Reluctant to share the news with Omama just yet, he walks a few blocks on the route of their daily walks to the narrow strip of St. Stephen's Park, named for Hungary's first king and its patron saint. He sits on a bench in the sun and stares unseeing at water splashing in a tall fountain adorned with stone cherubs. His ragged breath gradually grows more even; the pounding of his heart slows. He wills himself not to think of what just happened, but of the future. An hour passes, maybe two, and an idea begins to form in his mind. The sun drops below the crest of the hill to the west, and he stands and turns toward home. On the way, he meets my father, who, though shell-shocked, managed to finish the afternoon at work.

They open the gate and walk into the house. My mother and Omama are setting out a light supper of tea, crusty bread, and cheese on the dining room table. Omama's blue eyes are filled with concern at Opapa's sagging shoulders, his weary expression. She touches his arm gently, a question. "Elvették" (They took it), he says, slumping down on one of the chairs.

"Jaj, Istenem" (Oh, my God), she says. During their thirty-seven years of marriage, she raised the children and ran the household so Opapa could concentrate on his passion, the factory. What will this do to him?

For a few moments, Omama's words hang in the air, articulating the dread they all feel. They exchange stricken looks.

"What now?" my mother asks, breaking the silence.

"You and I still have jobs," my father says. "They must have been afraid to go too far."

"With the baby coming, I can't work much longer, but maybe you should quit, too," she says to my father.

"No," Opapa says quietly. "Who knows what else they'll do if you don't cooperate?" But he is free of the Communists' rules. "I'll start over," he says and outlines his plan to produce small household and farm implements on his own.

Omama mentions the modest income from her share of the Austrian textile factory and lumber mill her father left to his seven children. And they have always lived within their means. The family will survive. But already, the lives they know are slipping into the past.

Opapa would carry out his plan, setting up shop in space he rented from a locksmith. At the factory, the Communists would strip my father of his management position, relegate him to a make-work job collecting data, slash his pay in half. He would become a pariah. But it was a scheme my mother devised as she lay sleepless in her bed, mulling over the catastrophic events of the day, that likely prevented more dire consequences. She probably didn't share her plan with my father; his tendency to avoid conflict might have led him to try to stop her.

"My Russian father is friends with some of the Soviets," she declared at work the day after the takeover, within earshot of the office gossip. Perhaps she was exaggerating, but unlike most citizens, my Nagypapa *was* able to converse with the Soviets who occupied the country and supported the Communist takeover. "If something bad happens to us, they'll go after Ihász," she went on, confident that her words would soon find their way to the factory's new head. She then asked Nagypapa to bribe one of the Soviets he knew for a favor. A uniformed Soviet officer arrived at the factory a day or two later and asked for my father. When he appeared, the officer handed him an official-looking envelope. A jittery Ihász watched. The envelope might have contained instructions for reporting him to the Soviets if he mistreated my parents, or a declaration of support for my parents in the event of trouble at the factory. Ihász had no way of knowing that the envelope was in fact empty. The incident seemed to verify for him my mother's prediction—that if he gave my parents any trouble, the Soviets would protect them and punish him. He left my parents in peace.

* * *

I was born a month later, on April 24. The date was a Saturday in a town whose name, Szombathely, means "Saturday place," a reference to the open-air market where farmers from the surrounding area sold plums and dried peppers, eggs and sour cream, live chickens and geese. Of my birth, my mother said only that she labored on a bed with crisp white linens and a red satin comforter from morning until midafternoon. I drew my first breath in Omama and Opapa's house, in a bedroom overlooking the factory so recently wrested from my grandfather.

Would my parents forever connect my birth to what they had lost? Or did they, as trauma victims often do, find hope and comfort in the birth of a child? I never asked. Could any parent acknowledge that their child reminds them of one of their life's most devastating experiences? Instead, I tried putting myself in their place—a couple adjusting to each other, to marriage, to parenting Judy together—when forces beyond their control shattered their future. And then, a newborn baby. At best, my birth must have been bittersweet.

On May 14, when I was just three weeks old, the Communists fired my father. Perhaps they were weary of his presence, a constant reminder that the factory rightfully belonged to his family. He searched for work in similar firms, even as far away as Budapest. Everywhere, the same question: "Are you a member of the Communist Party?"

"No," my father answered. They said it didn't matter. But it did matter.

Whenever my parents went out to dinner, the same blond young man in civilian clothes materialized at a table nearby. They dined on chicken *paprikás* and butter lettuce salad; he nursed a glass of wine and watched them. If they caught his gaze, he nodded politely. He never left before they did. Several times, a jeep emblazoned with a red cross parked in front of Omama and Opapa's house. Everyone knew that such jeeps, though resembling Red Cross vehicles, actually belonged to the ÁVO, the Secret Police. My father worried that the ÁVO wouldn't stop at intimidation. He worried that their next move would be a rap on the door in the middle of the night, a common practice with people considered "class aliens," bringing exile to a remote village, imprisonment, or death.

My parents were determined to avoid that fate. At meals around Omama and Opapa's dining room table, my father argued for escape. "They're closing in on us. We have to go," he said.

"How can we leave everything we know?" Opapa asked.

"It would be too hard for older people like us," Omama added.

One night, my father's sister, Marianne, and her husband and two teenage sons joined the family for dinner. "What are we waiting for?" she asked.

But in the end, after sleepless nights debating the pros and cons in the darkness of their bedroom, only my parents were willing to act. The prospect of leaving their loved ones behind tormented them, but staying in Hungary would be even more intolerable.

* * *

In June 1948, my father decided we could wait no longer. A chimney sweep he knew led him to a border patrol sergeant who smuggled people to Austria. My father eyed the khaki-clad man warily from across a table. The sergeant, no doubt accustomed to skepticism from prospective clients, volunteered that if people wanted to leave Hungary, he believed they should be able to go. By helping them, he was earning extra money to finance his children's education. A mutually beneficial arrangement. He seemed sincere.

"How much?" my father asked.

"Two thousand forints," the sergeant replied. His fee, payable in advance, was more than my father made in a month before the factory takeover. And it would cover only crossing the border. When they arrived in Austria, my parents would be on their own.

Germany had annexed German-speaking Austria during World War II. In 1945, the victorious Allies—the United

States, Britain, France, and the Soviet Union—partitioned the country into four sectors, beginning a ten-year occupation. The eastern sector, next to the border with Hungary, was controlled by the same Soviets behind the Communist takeover. Omama's relatives there could help with transportation and shelter, but they were no guarantee against the Soviets, who actively hunted escapees from Hungary and sent any they caught back to the ÁVO. Our family would be safe only at our final destination, Rohrbach an der Lafnitz, in the British sector, twenty-five miles inside Austria. The facts distressed my father, but time was running out. He agreed to the man's terms.

The sergeant considered various escape options, finally deciding on a family picnic in the countryside near the border. After the meal, after my parents gathered up the remnants, he would guide the family across. He set no date. We would go when he deemed the conditions favorable.

Meanwhile, my father brooded. Could he trust the sergeant? Was his plan sound? He decided to consult a clairvoyant. She was the widow of a colonel in the pre-Soviet Hungarian Army and could be entrusted with his secret. The tall, elderly woman ushered my father into her apartment near the railroad station. "I'm planning to escape with my family," he told her. "Will we get out of Hungary safely?" The clairvoyant shut her eyes and was silent for a few moments. "Yes," she said. My father left, relieved.

The subject of the clairvoyant arose late in my questioning of my father. He mentioned her almost as an afterthought in one of our living room discussions. Learning of this consultation, so out of character for the serious, rational person I knew, underscored for me how wrenching the decision to escape must have been, how laden with anxiety and doubt.

Soon after my father's meeting with the seer, the sergeant contacted him. A complication. We couldn't go as a family after all; it would look too suspicious. He would take my father and Judy across the border on June 21, and my mother, carrying me, the next day.

My parents took a final stroll together around Szombathely on Sunday evening, June 20. From their neighborhood on the town's west side, they crossed over the Perint River, their backs to the setting sun. They passed whitewashed terra-cotta-roofed houses on Petőfi Sándor utca, namesake of the revered nineteenth-century poet, champion of the freedom and self-determination Hungary was rapidly losing under the Communists. Two miles across town, they paused at the Renaissance-style railroad station, its central turreted building flanked by two low wings with arched windows. In front, a cluster of perhaps twenty people sat on suitcases: children, young adults, gray-haired men and women. Ashen, anxious faces. Guarding them were two soldiers carrying rifles. The group had been captured at the border as they tried to escape.

The sight unnerved my parents. They later tried to calm themselves with white wine spritzers on the patio of the Mega Pince, a favorite bistro, next to the Gyöngyös, a stream named for pearls. Rustling trees, a darkening sky. Lights twinkled on in buildings that would soon exist only in their memories. A black-clad Gypsy band entertained with melancholy strains from fiddles and a cimbalom, a Hungarian dulcimer. My father requested a ballad, "Itt Hagyom a Falutokat" ("I'm Leaving Your Village") and, as was the custom, sang along:

I'll soon leave your village,
I'm traveling to a foreign land,
I'll say goodbye on a dark, moonless night,
So no one will see my tears.

Speak no ill of me for leaving,
I meant no one any harm,
You can blame me for nothing,
Except, perhaps, loving you.

Their stalker from the ÁVO sat at a nearby table, watching and listening. My mother was terrified that he would catch on and arrest them. Perhaps my father felt compelled to display that bravado to bolster his and my mother's courage—to dampen their fear, to strengthen their resolve, to erase from their minds the faces at the railroad station.

chapter three

Escape

The prospect of leaving Hungary separately, without the solace of each other's presence, only increased my parents' anxieties as the hours ticked closer to my father's departure with Judy on June 21. What was it like for them to part, not knowing if they would make it safely across the border with the child in their charge? Not knowing if the family would ever be reunited? Even as summer began on that warm, sunny morning, a chapter was ending. My father, in shirt-sleeves, pedaled away from Omama and Opapa's house on a battered bicycle he had borrowed from a teenage nephew, five-year-old Judy perched between him and the handlebars. The sergeant rode on a bicycle alongside them. The only possession my father carried with him was his wallet—no suitcase, no toys for Judy, no traces of the past. Judy, her blonde hair bobbed, wore her yellow dress sprinkled with daisies.

My parents had told her nothing, for fear she would blurt out their plans to someone who couldn't be trusted. Only at the last minute had they taken her to Vasvár to say goodbye to our maternal grandparents: petite, dark-haired Nagymama with her ready smile, and Nagypapa, outwardly gruff, but devoted to his granddaughter. Judy remembers little about that goodbye, my parents didn't describe to me the limited goodbyes they said to minimize our risk of exposure, and I was too young to say goodbye to anyone. I could only imagine all the goodbyes, both spoken and unspoken, that marked the end of our lives in Hungary.

I picture Nagymama and Nagypapa's first-floor apartment in a row house in Vasvár on the day of Judy and my parents' last visit. My parents chat with them at their dining room table, reminding them in low voices that, if anyone asks, they should deny any advance knowledge of our escape for their own protection.

"We'll send word as soon as possible if we make it out safely," my father says.

"Try not to worry about us in the meantime," my mother adds.

Judy hovers on the periphery, skipping around the rooms where she has spent so much of her young life, looking out the lace-curtained window at the grassy yard behind the house where she plays in warm weather. She sidles up to Nagypapa, who puts his arm around her and pulls her close. "Such a pretty girl," he says in Hungarian, with a heavy Russian accent. She leans against him, her head on his shoulder.

"We have to go," my mother says.

Judy turns toward her mustached grandfather. "Goodbye," she says, first to him, then to Nagymama. To her, this parting is no different from those at the end of her many visits.

"Goodbye, Jutkica," they respond, using a loving nickname for her, only too aware that this goodbye is final. They kneel on the floor to get as close as possible to their cherished first grandchild. Nagypapa hugs her, then Nagymama, then

Nagypapa again, each hug longer than the last. Finally, they clutch her at the same time, rocking her between them, not wanting to let go. They start to weep, Nagymama wailing in a high-pitched voice, Nagypapa muffling his grief behind a handkerchief.

Puzzled, Judy studies her grandparents' tearstained faces. "Why are you crying?"

"We have to go," my mother repeats before they can answer. Her own eyes well up as she hugs and kisses her parents, knowing she may never see them again. Watching the adults' reactions, Judy starts to realize this parting is different. She gazes back at Nagymama and Nagypapa with longing as my parents take her hands and guide her from the house. The sounds of sobbing echo in their ears.

To then go on a bicycle trip with my father, whom she was only beginning to know and trust as a parent, and the sergeant, a stranger, must have disturbed her even more. But she was an obedient child. She didn't resist. She didn't ask questions.

Riding out of town in the vicinity of the factory, the trio encountered a factory employee, perhaps an ironworker my father had once supervised, walking to work.

"Jó napot" (Good day), my father greeted him, with forced heartiness. His sweating palms gripped the handlebars as he willed the man to believe that he was embarking on nothing more than a summer outing with his daughter and a soldier friend.

The man looked at him curiously. "Good day," he responded, not slowing his pace. Still, my father worried that he might report what he had seen: the former factory owner's son, not known for associating with military personnel, in the company of an army sergeant. Glancing over his shoulder at the man's back, he could see nothing to suggest that he would. And even if the man did tell someone, he reassured himself, he and Judy would likely be across the border by the time anyone caught up with them. He relaxed as they rode slowly up a hill to Szombathely's outskirts, until another employee appeared. My father tensed up, called out a greeting. Again, the man responded and kept walking.

My father and the sergeant pedaled to Austria on a road lined with cornfields and pastures interspersed with groves of deciduous trees and an occasional thatch-roofed stucco farmhouse. After several miles, they were stopped by a border guard. Perhaps he was tall, with steely blue eyes.

"Identify yourself," he barked. My father handed him his driver's license. "Your destination?" Responding exactly as the sergeant had instructed him, my father named a town still in Hungary. The guard studied the license, gazed into my father's eyes, studied the license again. Was he in collusion with the sergeant, simply going through the motions? Or was he in fact weighing whether to send my father and Judy back to the ÁVO? After several excruciating minutes—minutes during which my father prayed that the clairvoyant he'd consulted knew her business—the guard allowed them to pass.

Two hours after setting out, they skirted the village of Pornóapáti and crossed a meadow to the border, the Pinka River. A footbridge spanned the narrow, ditch-like channel. An Austrian guard patrolled the far side. My father, fluent in German, translated as the sergeant engaged the friendly man in conversation. Soon, the guard waved my father and Judy on to Austria as the sergeant turned back to Hungary.

With my father speaking German and Judy remaining silent, they were able to pass as Austrians riding the six miles to Grosspetersdorf, where they spent the night at the home of a distant relative. The next day, another relative drove them fourteen miles to the home of Omama's sister-in-law in Pinkafeld, a haven where they would wait for my mother and me.

The next morning, my twenty-four-year-old mother donned a white blouse, a navy blue jacket, and a matching print skirt, an outfit a young matron might wear to run errands around town. She swathed me in a white bunting and cradled me in her arms. By seven thirty, she and the sergeant stood on the street near Omama and Opapa's house, waiting for the bus to the border. He guarded her lone brown suitcase. Numerous factory employees trudged past them en route to work. Most averted their eyes; no one greeted my mother. "After the takeover, they shunned me as if I had leprosy," she had told me sadly. A more pressing concern: did they suspect she was fleeing the country? Most of them knew the destination of the bus that stopped there. She dismissed the thought. No sane person would try to escape carrying a two-month-old baby.

I slept, oblivious. I was leaving the only environment I knew—my grandparents' house; their creased, smiling faces bending over me; the dapple of sunlight streaming through lace-curtained windows; the honeyed fragrance of locust blossoms outside our door; the ever-present buzz of the factory—and would remember nothing.

On the bus, my mother chose a window seat. She had no desire to talk to the sergeant, whom she considered mercenary. Instead, she watched Szombathely's buildings give way to the same green fields my father and sister had passed the day before. Perhaps she glanced at my slumbering face, stroked wisps of my blonde hair. She tried not to think about the captured escapees at the railroad station.

An hour later, the bus lumbered into Pornóapáti, a cluster of wretched houses. The sergeant guided my mother to one of them, the dirt-floored home of a middle-aged peasant couple. He handed them the suitcase. It contained little of value, just changes of clothing for each of us, some linens, and towels. "Why are you giving it to them?" my mother asked, dismayed at the prospect of losing even what little she had been able to bring.

"It would attract attention and make people suspicious," he answered. Better to leave it behind. He promised to have it delivered when our family arrived at our final destination in Rohrbach. My mother wasn't convinced, but she had no choice. The sergeant then escorted her, clutching me, across the Pinka River on an unguarded bridge a mile or two from where he had guided my father and Judy across.

Another house, brick, with modern farm equipment in the yard. A couple, several children. Before he left, the sergeant instructed the husband to call Omama's brother in Pinkafeld and ask him to fetch us. My mother rested on a chair in the house, cuddling me in her lap. "They ignored us," she said of the family, an edge to her voice. Hours passed. No one came. The couple grew nervous about what might happen to them if they were caught harboring escapees from Hungary. They put us on a yellow postal bus to Oberwart, fourteen miles away. From there, a second bus would take us the five miles to Pinkafeld to join Judy and my father.

The Oberwart bus stopped in several villages en route. In

one, a dark-haired man a few years older than my mother boarded. He sat down beside us, studied my mother and me.

"Did you just cross the border?" he whispered in Hungarian. Startled, my mother met his gaze. How had he guessed? And why wasn't he speaking German? Was he a Soviet spy? Perhaps his eyes were kind. Perhaps he patted me gently.

"Is it that obvious?" she asked. She thought she had concealed her hesitation, her fear.

The stranger, who often traveled the route in his work as a roofer, was also bound for Pinkafeld, his home. "You'll be in danger in Oberwart," he said. "Soviet soldiers check the identity of everyone who gets on the Pinkafeld bus."

"Dear God," my mother said, bowing her head in despair. Had she gotten us this far, only to be sent back to the ÁVO in Hungary? "What can I do?" she asked.

"Come to my mother's house in Oberwart," the man answered. "You can take care of the baby and I'll figure out a way for you to get past the Soviets."

Entering the modest house on the main square with the man, my mother relaxed. His mother bore an amazing resemblance to her own mother, and she welcomed us warmly. She cooed over me as my mother fed me and changed my diapers. Her son considered various strategies to get us on the bus. By then, my mother trusted him completely. She would do whatever he suggested.

Within an hour, they were returning to the bus stop. My mother hung back half a block away as her companion joined the line of waiting passengers. He cleared the checkpoint manned by two Soviets and got on the bus, choosing a window seat on the near side. My mother, rocking me, watched the Soviets carefully inspecting each passenger's documents. She huddled near a building, trying to make herself less visible.

She waited as the door of the bus swung closed, as the motor rumbled to life, as the Soviets strolled away. When the wheels began to turn, she broke into a run. Waving frantically, she called the man's name, Willi. The bus shuddered to a halt. The door opened. My mother, holding me close, boarded.

Riding to Pinkafeld, my mother and her new friend marveled that his plan had succeeded. The bus driver had believed his claim that my mother was his wife, arriving late to join him with their infant daughter. The Soviets didn't notice the two last-minute passengers. At their journey's end, the man guided my mother to the relative's home where my father and Judy waited. "At the exact moment I saw your father, the man disappeared," my mother told me with a smile during my questioning. Had she only imagined him? A joyful reunion. With our arrival, "a big stone fell from my shoulder," my father said in his letter to me.

Just as two men at the factory, Ihász and Ligeti, set our flight in motion, two men facilitated its successful conclusion. One, an unnamed army sergeant with divided loyalties, smuggling people for money. He never delivered our suitcase, but he delivered us. What act of grace led my father to him while he still exercised caution in his duplicitous work, before arrogance, or greed, or carelessness drove him to guide too many people across the border at once? My parents later heard he was caught. No doubt he ended up in prison, or dead. The other, a roofer named Willi riding a bus. What made him willing to risk helping two strangers? Was that too an act of grace? My parents believed it was. I agree.

The next day, a friend drove Judy and me to Rohrbach, five miles away in the safety of the British zone. The Soviets didn't demand identity papers from children, but my parents were still at risk. They struggled for hours over hilly terrain and the thick underbrush of a forest—sweating and tired, on constant alert for soldiers patrolling the countryside—before they were finally free.

chapter four

Displaced Persons

My parents began a new life in Rohrbach, a sleepy town on the banks of the Lafnitz River, in the eastern foothills of the Alps. For me, it's as though my life began there, with my own earliest memories of Judy and me splashing in the shallows of the river on lazy summer afternoons and riding on a log that my parents pushed back and forth between them. We lived in a modest but comfortable apartment in a building dubbed "Mausburg" for the many mice that also inhabited it. My father supervised the physical plant of the lumber mill owned by Omama and her siblings. My mother gave birth to my brother, Robie, just a year and a day after I was born. Judy walked through a forest to school in Eichberg, a mile uphill from town, and I played and argued and made up with my friend Liselotte. At Christmas, a tinkling bell behind a closed door signaled that *Jézuska,* the baby Jesus, had left gifts—my favorite, a short-haired brown teddy bear with beaded eyes and a ring in his left ear that became my constant companion. Our tree was decorated with white candles, silver ornaments, and Hungarian *szalon cukor*, candy wrapped in silver foil and white fringed tissue paper. Within the rhythms of daily life, the tension that had dominated my parents' lives since the takeover of the Reich Gépgyár began to dissipate, to drift away like wisps of smoke.

But eight months after we arrived in Austria, the calm was shattered by devastating news from Hungary. Opapa had awakened one day with a fever. His doctor could find no cause, but later dispatched a nurse to his house. She administered an injection. Within seconds, my grandfather gasped for air, collapsed, and died.

"The Communists murdered him," my father declared when he told me the story. A shocking allegation. Perhaps Opapa had suffered an allergic reaction. Still, the circumstances did seem suspect. Admiration blended with my sadness as I imagined my grandfather, stripped of the factory he had built, hammering sheet metal into dustpans, spades, and hoes that he sold to the man who rented him space to work. He defied the Communists to the end. A conceivable motive for murder.

That same year, 1949, on Hungary's side of the border, the Soviet-backed Communist regime erected the barbed-wire fences, minefields, and guard towers of the Iron Curtain, reinforcing the ideological barrier they had established years earlier. Omama, Nagymama, Nagypapa, and other relatives we had left behind were now imprisoned. They wrote letters about shortages of food and medicine, about the regime's increasing oppression. My parents were relieved that we had avoided that fate, and they did what they could to help, sending money and medicine. At the same time, their fears of the Soviets they had eluded, stationed just five miles from Rohrbach, reignited. The rest of the world was slow to grasp the destructive effect of the Soviet presence in Eastern Europe. But eventually, the other countries occupying Austria—the United States, France, and Great

Britain—realized that they could no longer trust their former World War II ally. Fears grew widespread that the Soviets would overrun the rest of Austria, if not all of Europe. My parents dreaded the thought of reliving earlier traumas. They decided to try to emigrate to the United States.

The International Refugee Organization, formed to resettle the millions of Europeans displaced by World War II, was in charge of a process both lengthy and complex. My parents needed to convince the IRO that we were refugees from Hungary, not just emigrants; that we sought political asylum in the United States, not just a better life. Early on, my father fielded the questions of an official in Kapfenberg, a couple of hours from Rohrbach. What had happened in Hungary? Why had we escaped? What would happen if we returned? He answered as honestly as possible, and afterward, he and my mother waited anxiously for the result. *Petition denied.* My parents were crushed, but they were unwilling to give up. My father wrote the organization a long letter in hopes of persuading officials to reverse their decision. In it, he detailed our family's hardships starting with the factory takeover. He enumerated the many reasons that Hungary was no longer the free country that some officials, at least, still seemed to believe it was. Weeks later, another letter arrived from the IRO. *Petition approved.*

There were more hurdles, more trips to Kapfenberg, and even to Salzburg, 250 miles away. We spent hours in waiting rooms crowded with people as desperate to leave Europe as my parents were—individuals and families with crying babies like Robie, on my mother's lap, and children like Judy and me, bored and restless, wandering around the room. One of the IRO's main objectives was to determine if we were sound of body. We stood in lines culminating in chest x-rays, blood draws, poking and prodding by doctors. My parents were also required to certify that they would be self-supporting in the United States and not rely on public assistance of any kind. The examinations, the meetings, and the waiting dragged on for three years. In the meantime, my parents were in limbo, living in Rohrbach, but longing to be in the United States, free of the Soviets' reach, free to build a life for their children that was safe and secure.

Clearance to leave Europe for the United States finally arrived in late 1951. My parents filled a pair of pale green, three-foot-tall wooden trunks with possessions we had accumulated in Rohrbach, among them a pink checked dress and felt toy dog my mother had sewn for me, Judy's school papers, Robie's diapers, a brown plaid fringed blanket, two red satin down comforters with white cotton covers, a green photo album with a white edelweiss blossom painted on its cover, my parents' German and Hungarian books. Bold black letters on the trunks spelled out my father's name in Hungarian, "Reich Sándor" (Alexander Reich) and "Church World Service, 120 East 23rd Street, New York 10 New York," the sponsor that would help us get settled in the United States.

We were scheduled to depart by boat from Bremerhaven, Germany. As we waited there in a refugee camp, my father was called in for more questioning, this time by the US Army. What was the layout of the former Reich Gépgyár? Where were other landmarks in Szombathely located? He was given no reasons for the questioning. Perhaps the army was preparing for potential military action behind the Iron Curtain. Or perhaps it was simply a final test. Regardless, my father's answers satisfied his interrogators.

* * *

We sailed on February 2, 1952, on the *General Sturgis*, a decommissioned World War II troop ship overflowing with fellow refugees longing for a life of freedom in America. Ours was the last group processed by the IRO before it was replaced by the United Nations High Commissioner for Refugees. The ship entered the North Sea and sailed southwestward through the English Channel, past the White Cliffs of Dover gleaming in morning sunlight, with no hint of the conditions that awaited on the North Atlantic. Twelve storm-tossed days. Tight quarters, minimal privacy. Rolling decks. Numerous retching passengers were confined to their beds, among them my mother and Judy. Nearly four years old, I spent most of the crossing with my father and Robie and the teddy bear that I carried everywhere, from the dormitory-like sleeping quarters with curtained-off bunks, to the decks with their view of leaden skies and the endless peaks and troughs of the turbulent, white-capped ocean. The crossing was an interlude lived in the moment, with little time for thought, for regret, for worry about the future.

We docked in New York City on February 14, two days after the third anniversary of Opapa's death. Church World Service informed my parents we would be going to Chicago, where a job as an ironworker awaited my father. While they finalized the arrangements, we waited a few blocks from their office at the Chelsea Hotel on West Twenty-Third Street, a twelve-story brick building with rows of narrow sash windows fronted by ornate ironwork. We didn't know then that the hotel giving us our first glimpse of American life had once hosted Mark Twain and that it would become well-known as a haven for writers, artists, musicians, and actors, both famous and infamous, including Dylan Thomas and Arthur Miller and Janis Joplin. To us, the Chelsea was simply a way station to a new life whose shape was still obscure. In the meantime, my father obtained status reports from our sponsor, and my mother cooked meals on a hotplate in our room, and we strolled the streets around the hotel and sometimes roamed farther afield to the open spaces of Central Park.

The job offer in Chicago was eventually withdrawn. We continued to wait as our sponsor scrambled to find another destination for us. My father met with their staff one day and returned to the Chelsea with a question for my mother. "How would you like to go to Billings, Montana?"

"Where is that?" she asked. My parents had at least heard of Chicago and Cleveland and other eastern cities with enclaves of Hungarian refugees. Billings, Montana was an unknown. To later learn that it was two-thirds of the way across the United States, farther than ever from Hungary in the wide-open spaces of the West, did not reassure them. Church World Service proposed Billings because First Congregational Church there had already sponsored several refugee families, and, with some prodding, agreed to take one more. My parents still had their doubts. But they had no choice.

We left New York's Penn Station on the Pennsylvania Railroad the afternoon of March 6. The next day, we changed trains in Chicago, the city that, but for a twist of fate, might have become our new home. Farther west in St. Paul, Minnesota, we transferred to the Northern Pacific train that would take us to Billings. More than twenty-four hours later, near midnight on March 8, 1952, we pulled into the yellow brick station on the east side of Billings, the surrounding air bathed in the stench of the nearby stockyards. The darkness revealed little, but my parents felt as though we had been deposited in the middle of nowhere. Our train had chugged for hours through the Great Plains of North Dakota and eastern Montana, the towns and farms dotting their sagebrushed flatness growing sparser the farther west we traveled. Billings, population fifty thousand, was the largest city for hundreds of miles, similar in size to Szombathely. But there the resemblance ended.

The next day revealed an arid landscape that was almost surreal. Rimrocks—yellow-brown sandstone cliffs five hundred feet tall, their tops and ledges dotted with ponderosa pines—dominated the north side of the city and extended westward for many miles. Another section jutted southeastward, parallel to the Yellowstone River. The city, with its downtown of two- and three-story buildings and neighborhoods on both sides of the railroad tracks, rested in a valley open to the southwest where, sixty miles away, the snowcapped Beartooth Mountains floated like a mirage. The trees were bare and the grass was dry in late winter, infusing the entire city with the drab shades of the Rims. But the sky, dotted with puffy cumulus clouds, was azure blue, and extended in all directions as far as the eye could see.

Jackie and Stewart North represented First Congregational Church as our sponsors. They met us at the train that first night and helped ease us into our new life. Jackie was in her early forties, a striking woman with pale skin and auburn hair pulled back in a severe bun. The suede jackets, straight skirts, and high-heeled pumps she wore gave her an aura of wealth and glamour. An organizer who knew how to get things done, she issued opinions and directives in a nasal voice. Her portly insurance-broker husband, with thick glasses and thinning gray hair, was more than a decade older. He was as reserved as his wife was outgoing and was content to let her take the lead.

Our new home was a small white rental house with a red roof on Rimrock Road, near the foot of the sandstone cliffs for which the street was named. The neighborhood, a couple of miles from downtown, was semirural, with houses far grander than ours scattered on large lots. With the help of others from the church, Jackie and Stewart furnished our house, stocked our refrigerator, gave advice, helped enroll Judy in school and my parents in English language classes, and found work for my parents—my father as a machinist at Reimer's Machine Shop, my mother as a cleaning lady at Deaconess Hospital. My parents had scant experience needing or accepting so much help from strangers, but they were grateful.

They also found comfort in the handful of other Hungarian refugee families in town, with whom they could speak their native language and reminisce about their homeland. Still, they weren't prepared for the sniping and jockeying for help and resources that sometimes occurred among them, or for their boasting about former lives in Hungary as army officers and aristocrats. As if that meant anything in the United States. My parents, modest people who understood that their new life was a blank slate, avoided talking with their new friends about their former lives and the Reich Gépgyár.

It was a minor incident, but one with a powerful impact on my mother's outlook as we settled in Billings. More familiar with the outcome than the details, I imagine what happened in order to try to understand how my mother began to feel insecure, to avoid risk, to become someone other than the courageous woman who escaped from Hungary with me in her arms. Whether she intended to do so or not, she transmitted some of that newfound timidity to me, complicating my own tightrope walk between my Hungarian and American worlds.

I try to put myself in my mother's place at the gathering of perhaps ten or fifteen women, all Americans except for my mother and her friend, Klári, a Hungarian refugee who had arrived in Billings with her family a couple of years before we did. They're having coffee at the gracious home of a woman named Virginia, wife of a doctor, who with her husband is a prominent member of First Congregational Church. My mother's blue eyes dart around the circle of women drinking coffee and eating pastries. She tries to discern from their facial expressions, their gestures, their clothes, what the norms are, what is accepted and valued in this country where so much is different from what she was accustomed to in Hungary and Austria. Following the flow of the conversation about children and husbands and shopping is still a struggle for her and she sometimes whispers to Klári, asking her to interpret what someone has said.

She studies the tailored dress one of the women is wearing. As an accomplished seamstress, she wonders if she could copy the dress if she found the right pattern, if she put a little money aside from her earnings, if she spent some nights at her Singer treadle sewing machine after long days cleaning hospital rooms. It would give her something to look forward to, something to take her mind off the fact that every time she opens her mouth and says something, people immediately know that she's a refugee, a displaced person, a DP. "Where are you from?" they ask. Maybe they're being kind; maybe they truly want to know. But why should she, as private as she is, be required to reveal her life story to anyone who asks? All she wants to do is to fit in, to be able to be herself without this constant scrutiny.

Her attention drifts back to Irma, a trim woman with short, curly salt-and-pepper hair who is talking to the group. Her husband owns a successful car dealership, and they live in a house with a swimming pool. "I'm having a party in a couple of weeks," she announces brightly as the get-together winds down. The women stand and gather their belongings, chatting among themselves. Irma approaches each cluster. "Please come," she says, adding the specifics of date and time. When she catches sight of my mother and Klári, she turns and walks away. Her message is clear. The refugees in the group are not welcome. My mother feels stung, humiliated. In Hungary before the factory takeover, she would have been eagerly sought after as a guest to such a party. Not anymore.

The snub triggers thoughts of other challenges she and my father face in this alien place. Trying to make themselves understood in English despite thick accents. Being forced to rely on their daughters to speak for them in a role reversal both unfamiliar and unwelcome. Dealing with schools and banks and stores and their employers, never fully comprehending, never fully able to express themselves. And raising three children with the growing dread that something is terribly wrong with one of them.

chapter five

Robie

As a blond, chubby-cheeked child of four, my brother, Robie, didn't speak. He had started learning to talk, but his progress stopped when he was two. "Kong … kong … kong," he intoned instead in a singsong voice, flapping his hands and skinny forearms in excitement. Sometimes his arms and face turned rigid, his round blue eyes staring in apprehension at a threat only he could see. Or he burst into gales of laughter at jokes evident only to himself. He seemed to be in his own world as he scribbled aimlessly on sheets of typing paper with pencils or crayons, and few toys interested him. But he was fascinated by a set of flat wooden tiles in primary colors that he used to create designs so intricate that, years later, a family friend still remembered them. And he loved trains. Wooden trains that he pulled on the edge of our kitchen table with its yellow Formica top, and passenger and freight trains rolling on the tracks that bisected Billings. "Choo-haha, choo-haha!" he cried whenever he heard the blare of a train whistle. And he was restless, often in motion. On the rare occasions that he sat still, he never looked directly at anyone. He gazed past our faces, as though he could see a future that didn't include his family.

He was most comfortable with my mother. She had a volatile temper, but was always gentle with him, anticipating his every want and need. "Édes kicsi fiam" (My sweet little son), she crooned as she held him on her lap, hugging and kissing him. No matter how hard she worked, she was never too tired to help him eat, get dressed, go to the bathroom, fall asleep. Judy, too, reserved her gentler side for Robie, and he let her and my mother caress him as much as they wanted. My father, a perfectionist who liked order in his life, seemed bewildered by his only son, so different from the one he had imagined. He stayed in the background. And I, too young to fully understand, just accepted him as part of the landscape of my childhood. With our birthdays just a year and a day apart, I thought of him as my almost-twin. We celebrated together.

A black-and-white snapshot from April 1955 shows us sitting side by side at our kitchen table covered with a white cloth and our good china, decorated with lilies of the valley. Robie's hair is darker than it was when he was younger, his face thinner. Seven candles burn on my *dobos torta*, a yellow cake filled with chocolate buttercream frosting, and six on his chocolate pie edged with whipped cream. Also on the table are a gift-wrapped package for each of us. His, bulky, perhaps a truck. Mine, flat, probably a book. We both smile at the camera, but I sit straight in my blouse and pastel cardigan, my hands folded in my lap. Robie rests his chin on his plate.

By then, we had moved from Rimrock Road to a housing project originally built for the families of servicemen returning from World War II. When we arrived, the neighborhood covering the 800 block of Avenues E and F was home to a wide range of families who needed affordable housing, including professionals and government workers. But they gradually drifted away, replaced by poorer families. Living there began to carry a stigma. Still, we liked being closer to downtown and the hilly, wooded expanse of Pioneer Park, where Judy, Robie, and I sledded in winter and played on the merry-go-round and swings in the summer. Our one-story, white wood frame house was identical to all the other houses on our side of Avenue E: no more than eight hundred square feet, with two bedrooms, a tiny bath with a shower, a living room, and a kitchen barely large enough to accommodate the table that held Robie's and my birthday cakes and gifts. The other houses were pastel-colored duplexes with front doors next to one another and log cabins painted dark shades of red and green. Beside our house was a sloping dirt and gravel driveway that led to a small garage. The backyard, dominated by a clothesline on which my mother hung our weekly wash with wooden clothespins, was bordered by a city landfill where we liked to climb on the mounds of dirt. Once a week, our landlord, Mr. Lutzker, a squat man with gray, slicked-back hair and a cigar clamped between his lips, cruised slowly through his domain in his shiny pink Cadillac. We children watched him from the side of the road, awed.

One summer day a couple of months after Robie's and my birthday celebration, my parents called me into the living room. "Your father and I have to leave for a couple of hours," my mother said in Hungarian. An important errand. Judy, away for the afternoon, wasn't available to babysit. My parents couldn't afford to hire a sitter, and, in any case, would have been reluctant to entrust Robie's care to someone outside the family.

"Can we come?" I asked.

"No," my mother said.

"Why not?"

"Because I said so."

"Do I have to take care of Robie?" I asked.

"Yes," my father said, his tone pleading. He knew how defiant I could be and wanted to avoid a confrontation.

"I don't want to," I said, sullen, crossing my arms in front of my chest.

"You must," my mother said. Her stern expression warned she wouldn't tolerate further arguing.

"You'll be fine; just keep the door locked," my father said. He pointed to the deadbolt, operated with a knob on the paneled front door that led to our square front porch. My mother kneeled down and hugged Robie, pressing her face to his hair. She turned to me. "Do not go outside or let anyone in, do you understand?"

"Okay ..." I answered, my lip quivering. My father smiled at me in encouragement. Wanting to seem brave, I smiled back. But as the door closed behind my parents, my stomach fluttered with anxiety.

Robie lounged awkwardly against an arm of the sofa and wailed at our mother's departure. "It's okay," I said with false confidence, patting his arm. "Let's play with your tiles." Retrieving the box from a shelf, I sank down on the floor and pulled him next to me. "Look, Robie!" I said, spreading the tiles on the brown tweed carpet. He studied them, his distress forgotten. His hands flapped as I rested my hand on his back in a subtle effort to keep him near me. He picked out a tile and laid it in an open space; then, next to it another, and then another. For a few precious minutes, he was enthralled, his head bent down, totally focused on his task. A colorful, star-like design began to emerge. "That's beautiful!" I exclaimed. But before long, my brother's wiry body strained against my arm. Suddenly, he swept his hands under the tiles and scattered them all over the room—by the desk where my mother typed letters to Hungary, by the mahogany upright Kimball piano that Judy played, by the easy chair where my father read books about yoga and Eastern religions. "Oh, no!" I cried. Grasping Robie's arm with one hand, I scooped up the tiles and placed them back in the box. His eyes darted around the room and landed on the front door. Freeing himself from my grasp, he rushed to it and started to turn the knob on the deadbolt.

"No, Robie," I said as I grabbed him and half-pushed, half-pulled him into our bedroom. I found his wooden train. We sat down on the floor, and he ran it in circles in the open space between Judy's and my twin beds on either side of the room. Near the foot of my bed was the crib where he, still small for his age, slept. But in a few minutes, as suddenly as he had abandoned the tiles, he thrust the train aside with a clatter. He jumped up and darted back to the living room. Again, he went to the door and tried to unlock it.

I hovered near him, determined to keep him in the house. He turned the knob to the open position. I turned it back and tugged his hand away. He used his other hand. I pulled him back from the door. Arms swinging at me, he rushed back. We scuffled for several minutes. Then, without warning, the door flew open. Robie shot out of the house, onto the porch, and down the two stairs. In seconds, he was halfway down the street. "Come back, Robie!" I yelled. He ignored me. I thought about trying to follow him, but I knew it would be useless. He was too fast. It didn't occur to me to go to the neighbors, to the Gertzes or the Reids or the Moras, and ask for their help. My parents hadn't suggested that option, perhaps because they didn't anticipate an emergency, or they wanted to avoid involving the neighbors in our problems. Defeated, I shuffled back into the house and locked the door. I sat on the sofa and, filled with dread, waited for my parents to come home.

When they did, my mother looked around the room. "Where's Robie?" she asked.

"He ran away," I answered. "I tried, but I couldn't stop him."

"How could you … ?" she began, glowering, her arm raised. I cringed.

"Leave her alone," my father said, putting his hand on my shoulder. "We need to find Robie."

The police were called; the situation explained. And then, the excruciating wait to find out what had happened to him. My parents and I said little, lost in our own imaginings, our own scenarios of disaster. When Judy came home and learned what had happened, she looked at me in disgust.

A police cruiser eventually pulled up in front of our house. Curious neighbors stood at their windows and on the street, staring. Robie, grinning, emerged from the back seat wrapped in an olive-drab army blanket, oblivious to the worry he had caused. The policemen explained that they had found him wandering a mile away, at Evergreen Shopping Center. Naked. He had shed his shirt and pants and underwear along the way. Back in the house, after my mother had fussed over him, I hugged him, relieved that he wasn't hurt. My parents didn't punish me, but I couldn't help feeling that they blamed me for what had happened. I blamed myself. And I was also embarrassed. For him. For all of us.

* * *

That day, my parents' hopes for Robie collided with a reality that had begun a couple of years earlier, when Jackie, our sponsor, had helped them find a psychologist to evaluate him. My mother had taken Robie to the appointment with Angela, another Hungarian refugee more proficient in English, to act as interpreter. The psychologist administered a battery of tests. The instructions were in English, of course, but Robie was accustomed to responding to us as we spoke in Hungarian. Angela, short and tense, with a dancer's posture, was a virtual stranger to Robie, not someone he would have trusted. Even if she understood the psychologist's instructions, it seems unlikely that she could have conveyed them to my brother in a way to elicit his best response. And my mother would have had difficulty helping with instructions she received secondhand. Regardless, when the psychologist was finished and had scored the tests, Angela, without preamble, translated his diagnosis: "A fiad egy idióta." (Your son is an idiot.)

Demeaning as it sounds in a modern context, the term was part of the official classification system for levels of mental retardation in the 1950s. My mother must have flinched at the words, at the pity she saw in Angela's eyes. But she would have been stoic, sweeping Robie into her arms and hugging him close. Only at home would she weep for what the diagnosis might mean for her youngest child. She raged at the humiliation of learning the devastating news from the lips of an acquaintance, because she didn't know enough English. My father comforted her, stroking her hair. But the scene must have taken place behind closed doors because I learned what happened much later. And many more years passed before we understood that Robie was in fact autistic. The psychologist may not have even known about a disorder identified in 1943, just a decade before the evaluation.

Robie's running away forced my parents to acknowledge that he needed more help than they, still struggling to adapt to a new country, could give him. In the 1950s, there were no special education programs in the schools, no community programs for the disabled, no counseling and support for parents. The only option available for my brother was a state institution, the Montana State Training School in Boulder, 250 miles from Billings. With Jackie's help, my parents reluctantly made plans to place him there.

On Robie's last day at home a few months later, I stood on the ragged edge of grass bordering the asphalt of Avenue E as my parents carried cardboard boxes from the house and loaded them in the trunk of Jackie's sleek dark sedan. In them were Robie's pants, shirts, and underwear that my mother had carefully marked with his name in permanent ink, and his beloved colored tiles and wooden trains. He danced around the yard, unaware that he was leaving us. My mother, in a navy blue coat with a white shawl collar, pulled him to her, speaking softly, trying to calm him. She was going with Jackie to help Robie get settled. Her heart must have been breaking as she contemplated the five-hour trip over two-lane roads—through the towns of Lavina and White Sulphur Springs and Townsend and over passes in the Big Belt and Elkhorn Mountains—that would separate her from her youngest child. But then, I didn't understand the effect that the distance would have not only on her, but on all of us.

"Goodbye, Robie," I whispered to him past the lump in my throat. My mother helped him into the back seat and took her place in the front next to Jackie. My father, Judy, and I stood waving as the car pulled away, Robie's small face visible in the window. Filled with a mixture of guilt and relief, I told myself he would only be gone awhile, that he would get help, that he would be back.

chapter six

Witness

THE AFTERNOON OF February 2, 1956, a few months after Robie left home, seemed no different from the end of any other school day. After the last bell rang, I strolled out of Mrs. McKelvie's second grade classroom in a crowd of other children, through halls covered in polished linoleum, and out the front doors of Highland Elementary School. I loved learning to read and write in that flat-roofed red brick building built the same year I was born and often hated to leave. Pausing on the front stairs, I felt the gentle breeze of one of those mild, sunny days in southern Montana that hint of spring. Snow starting to melt and turn soiled around the edges. Slushy pavement and patches of yellow grass. But as I turned toward home, two blocks away, I noticed our navy blue 1948 Chevrolet sedan parked at the curb with my parents sitting inside. My mother rolled down the window on the passenger side, closest to the sidewalk, and poked her head out. "Erika, come here!" she called in Hungarian. "You need to come with us." She slid out of the car and I ducked into the back seat, my cheeks flaming at the possibility that classmates had heard her and were staring at us, curious.

"Hello," my father said, also in Hungarian, smiling under his trim dark mustache.

"Hi," I said in English, sliding across the soft gray plush upholstery to sit behind him. I turned toward the window facing the street so that anyone who might be watching wouldn't recognize me. Soon Judy joined us. At thirteen, she should have been in junior high, but she was still at Highland because when she started school in Billings, she had been sent back two grades to learn English. She studied my parents with her wide-set blue eyes, as puzzled as I was.

"We're going to the South Side," my mother explained. The Bureau of Indian Affairs had hired my father, recently laid off from Eaton Metal, to repair the roof of a house there. Meticulous with any project he undertook, he wanted to inspect the roof before doing the work. If he did well, perhaps there would be other jobs.

"Why do Judy and I have to go?" I asked. "It sounds boring."

"Because we say so," my father answered, his tone uncharacteristically firm. My mother turned and glared at me. I decided not to argue.

We drove from the school past the hills of Pioneer Park, with its evergreens and vistas southward to the Pryor Mountains; through neighborhoods of stately colonials and tidy bungalows; into downtown, home of First Congregational Church, where we worshipped on Sundays, and Hart Albin's, a posh department store beyond our means; across the Northern Pacific railroad tracks that had brought us to Billings; to Minnesota Avenue, gateway to the South Side. The sun hung low in the sky, a flaming backdrop to bare trees casting long shadows over the neighborhood of dilapidated houses, the sugar beet factory, and bars and taverns where too much alcohol mixed with guns and knives late at night sometimes ended in tragedy. Poverty and prejudice relegated most of the town's Blacks, Mexicans, and Native Americans to the area, along with white people on the fringes. People like us. We could just as easily have landed there as in our housing project.

Perhaps all too aware of that fact, my parents avoided going there. Only on an occasional sweltering summer day did we cross the South Side on our way to Josephine Park, where we picnicked on bologna sandwiches and Hungarian pastries my mother made and washed it down with orange Nehi pop in the shade of huge cottonwood trees. Afterward, we skipped flat stones on the muddy surface of the Yellowstone River flowing lazily between the park and Sacrifice Cliff, part of the rimrocks dominating the north and east sides of town. Legends dating back to the 1700s tell of Crow warriors who killed themselves by plunging from the cliff on blindfolded ponies. In one version, they did so to appease the gods in hopes of halting a smallpox epidemic ravaging their people; in another, they were stricken with grief over the smallpox deaths of the women they loved. Even the edges of the South Side were tinged in melancholy.

A half hour after leaving my school, we were parked on the west side of South Twenty-Fourth Street, across from the house with the damaged roof. My parents' voices rose and fell as they discussed the repairs my father would make. Judy, locked in her own adolescent world, was silent; she and I often had little to say to each other. I stared out the window.

The house was a rectangular box covered in dingy, peeling white paint, its narrow end facing the street. Two steps led to a small stoop and a screen door loose on its hinges. Shingles were missing from the brown asphalt roof. Several men, some with black hair and coppery skin suggesting they were Native American, stood in the front yard, their voices a murmur. A few feet away from them stood a lone woman. Her long hair was also black, and she wore a red wool coat. She faced the house at the front edge of the yard, no more than thirty feet from us.

Soon, a second woman appeared in the doorway. She swung open the screen door and stepped outside. She could have been any age from thirty to fifty, her dumpy body clad in a drab housedress and shapeless sweater. A wild tangle of ash brown hair framed her round, pale face. In her right hand, at hip level, she grasped a rifle. She slowly lifted the rifle to her face and aimed it at the woman in the red coat. No one in the yard seemed to notice. Suddenly, a sharp *crack* reverberated through the air. A puff of smoke drifted from the end of the rifle barrel. The woman in red slumped to the ground, her coat a blood-like slash across the snow. The men yelled and scattered, then rushed to the woman's side and squatted around her. The woman at the doorway lowered the rifle, surveyed the scene without expression, turned, and walked back into the house. The screen door shuddered on its hinges.

I watched, spellbound. Was the woman dead? She lay motionless, but there was no sign of blood. What I had just witnessed seemed unreal, impossible. Not in daylight. Not in front of so many people. Not in front of us.

"She shot her!" my father exclaimed.

"I know," I replied. I felt numb. My mother and Judy had also seen at least part of what happened from the far side of the car, though perhaps in less detail. Seconds later, my parents exchanged a look and whispered to each other. My father started the car and began to ease it down the street.

"Are we just going to leave?" I asked.

"Yes," he answered. "There are plenty of witnesses."

"We don't need to be a part of this," my mother added.

"But we *are* a part of it," I argued. Unlike Judy, I never hesitated to share my opinions, whether or not my parents wanted to hear them. "We should go to the police."

"No," my father said.

"Why not? We could tell them what we saw."

"We're not telling anyone anything."

"I think we should."

"Stop it," my mother said, glaring at me for the second time that afternoon. I fell silent. As we drove home, I thought about death, a concept not unfamiliar to me, though only from a distance. The gray baby rabbit we had gotten for Easter that died a few weeks later. I had peered into its grass-lined box covered with chicken wire one morning before school and noticed that it lay very still. My parents convinced me that it was only sleeping. By the time I returned home and learned the truth, they had disposed of the body.

And a couple of years earlier, my mother's friend Irene had committed suicide. She was a plump, motherly woman from the church who had discussed politics with my mother and plied us children with chocolate chip cookies when we visited. She was also depressed. One day, sitting in front of her dressing table mirror with a pistol she had bought at a downtown pawnshop, she shot herself in the right temple. But my parents had left us children at home on the dark, stormy day of her service at Smith's Funeral Home. This time, death's skirts brushed much closer.

* * *

The next day, my mother pored over the account of the shooting in the *Billings Gazette.* "The woman didn't die," she reported. The bullet had hit her above her left eye, and doctors performed emergency surgery. I was relieved. I hoped that the woman would recover, that the incident we had so inadvertently stumbled upon would magically reverse itself like a movie rewinding, that our lives would revert to the way they had been before.

But two days later, we learned that the woman, in a semi-coma, paralyzed on her right side and unable to speak, had died. The county attorney later charged the shooter with first-degree murder.

"Now you really must keep quiet," my mother warned Judy and me.

"No one can know we were there," my father added.

Their grim faces told me they were serious, that there was a critical difference between a shooting and a murder, that the consequences if someone learned we had been witnesses and had not come forward could be grave.

"Okay," I agreed, though I still thought we should go to the police.

At the time, I didn't know the sordid details surrounding the shooting; my parents no doubt believed they were inappropriate to share with an eight-year-old child. But four decades later, I remembered the incident in a writing class and wanted to know more. I spent a sweltering summer afternoon during a visit to my parents poring over microfiche copies of the *Billings Gazette* in the local library to learn that the shooter had been a woman named Winnifred, married to the brother of the victim, Mary, a thirty-two-year-old mother of four who abused alcohol. Earlier in the day, Mary, drunk, had accused her sister-in-law of cheating on her husband. Winnifred had fervently denied the allegation. Tension between the bickering women grew with each passing hour, and Winnifred eventually called the police. They had investigated and advised the women to stay away from each other. But not long before we arrived on the scene, Mary returned to Winnifred's house. She tried to break in the back door. Winnifred had kept her out by wedging a knife in the doorjamb. Mary then went to the front yard, where we saw Winnifred shoot her. In the absence of those facts, I assumed the victim had simply been in the wrong place at the wrong time, gunned down without provocation. Had I known the truth and been able to talk with others, perhaps a counselor, about what I had seen, I might have avoided the fears and anxieties about death I felt in the weeks and months afterward.

My parents heeded their own counsel to keep quiet. Just days after the shooting, my father returned to the house and repaired the roof. If he encountered any of the men who had been standing in the yard that afternoon, he gave no sign that we had witnessed what had happened. My mother later discussed the upcoming trial over coffee with the wife of Winnifred's public defender, a young attorney just starting his career who lived on the next street over in our housing project. She and my mother mused about the odds of his gaining an acquittal for the shooter on his first-ever murder case. My mother never mentioned what we had seen. We all kept quiet—in the days leading up to the trial, during the trial, and even after Winnifred was acquitted of all charges and set free.

A year or so after I learned the details of the case, Judy mentioned that an attorney in the government office where she worked in Portland had lived in our housing project in Billings in the 1950s.

"Ask him if he knows anything about the murder we saw," I urged her. She did. It turned out he had been Winnifred's defense attorney. I traveled to Portland to meet him. A burly gray-haired man in his seventies, he recounted for me his involvement with his client. He used the cane he walked with to demonstrate the core of her defense—that she wasn't accustomed to handling a rifle and instead of scaring Mary, as she had intended, she had fumbled with the weapon and shot her by accident. He put me in touch with the prosecutor, still living in Billings, and I spoke with him by phone. In a quavering voice, he told me of errors he had made that caused him to lose the case.

I told both attorneys what we had seen. Both thought our testimony would likely have resulted in Winnifred's being convicted of murder, or at least manslaughter, and her doing time in prison. The men in the yard had been either unreliable or uncooperative as witnesses, and none had contradicted Winnifred's story. We would have been far more credible as bystanders testifying that Winnifred had aimed the rifle directly at the victim before she pulled the trigger, and had shown no shock or concern after the woman collapsed, clear indications that she intended to inflict bodily harm. I was dismayed to learn from the attorneys that our failure to step forward was indeed what enabled Winnifred to avoid legal consequences for her criminal act.

What did my parents fear? No doubt the prospect of becoming entangled in a complex legal system they didn't fully understand, conducted in a language they were still learning, gave them pause. So did the possibility that someone connected with the shooter might retaliate against us. There were also the racial overtones of a case involving a Caucasian perpetrator and a victim who was Native American. But it was more than that. My parents had risked everything to escape from a repressive Communist regime that punished noncompliant people with imprisonment or death. A regime they suspected had murdered my paternal grandfather. A regime that was holding millions of people, including our relatives, hostage behind the Iron Curtain. Keeping silent was a skill my parents had learned as a means to survive, a habit not easily broken.

chapter seven

Family Portrait

WITH OR WITHOUT Robie among us, we weren't an ordinary family. At least we weren't the kind of family I would have wanted—a family that banded together, us against the world, when challenges arose, as they often did in Billings. Instead, under that deep blue Montana sky, we functioned less as a unit than as pairs: my parents, when they weren't fighting; my mother and Judy; my father and me.

I seemed to have a knack for irritating my mother, but her temper erupted in full force most often toward my father, especially when he lost a job, a not-uncommon occurrence. He worked hard and did his best, but the transition from managing a hundred employees in his family's factory to taking orders from others in metal fabricating jobs in Billings was a major obstacle for him. "Mi bajod van?" (What's the matter with you?) my mother demanded the day he came home and told her he had lost his job at Eaton Metal. The energy that crackled from every pore of her five feet two inches grew even more intense, and her red-lipsticked mouth twisted in anger. Her voice grew louder and louder as she enumerated his faults, until all I wanted to do was run and hide in the bedroom I shared with Judy and plug my ears so I couldn't hear the barbs she was hurling at him.

"Ne, ne" (Don't, don't), my father answered. Always dignified, he held his hands with their long fingers raised in front of his body as though protecting himself from a physical attack, appealing for calm. But my mother raged on, her voice reverberating from the beige walls of our living room. Her frustration was understandable. She had left her cleaning job at Deaconess Hospital for the greater flexibility of self-employment. Rather than having help cleaning her own house, as she would have had in the married life she and my father had envisioned in Hungary, she was spending six days a week dusting and vacuuming and scrubbing the houses of the Kings, the Fanshawes, and the Blaines to make ends meet. Losing my father's income meant more financial struggles and drove her to the breaking point. Finally, spent, she stopped talking to him. He touched her arm, and she brushed it away. He greeted her, and she looked through him as though he weren't there.

Her silence crushed him. He coped by retreating to an Eastern philosophy book or hammering one of the sheets of copper from which he created decorative bowls. But after a day or two, he couldn't stand it anymore and sought me out. "Erikám," he began, using an affectionate Hungarian form of my name. "Please ask your mother if she'll make up with me."

"Ask her yourself," I wanted to say. But I loved my father, whose placid personality helped smooth the ups and downs of my own mercurial nature, and I hated to see him unhappy. I waited until my mother seemed receptive, and then went to her. She might have been relaxing on the roll-armed sofa covered in the tan slipcover she had sewed, smoking a cigarette and paging through *True Confessions*, a magazine that with its simple plot lines and sentence structure helped her learn to read English.

"Dad wants to make up with you," I said. My mother looked up at me, expressionless, as I stood before her, my schoolgirl's face hot with my father's humiliation. After a few moments that felt like an eternity, she relented.

"All right," she said, tossing her magazine aside. Soon, she and my father were talking and laughing and kissing again as though nothing had happened. The tension in our house eased—until the next time he lost a job or otherwise fell short of her expectations.

* * *

If things had been different, Judy and I might have commiserated over our parents' behavior. But she was five years older, which in and of itself created a certain distance between us. And she had her own problems: learning to speak English while adjusting to school in the United States, the discomfort of being two years older than her classmates. She also resented that my parents, of necessity, relied on her to care for Robie and me—and then, just me—in her free time after school and on weekends. Setting Judy off was as easy for me as touching a match to a fuse. I had a mind of my own and a smart mouth, and I didn't like her taking care of me any more than she liked doing it.

She was babysitting me one day when I moved toward the front door. "I'm going outside to play," I announced.

"Stay in here," Judy warned, hands on her slim hips,

shaking her head, her ponytail swinging from side to side. "I need to keep an eye on you."

"Make me," I said.

"Okay," she answered. Before I knew what was happening, I was thrashing around on the sofa, my arms flailing to fend off her blows.

"Stop it!" I wailed as she slapped at any part of my body that was exposed.

"Are you going to do what I tell you?" she asked, pausing in her assault. I was grateful for the respite, but I didn't answer right away.

"Maybe," I finally said, unwilling to concede total defeat.

"You'd better not tell Mom and Dad," she said, giving me a final whack. I never did. I worried that if I told and they punished her, she might actually hurt me the next time. Even as a child, I sensed that my parents were overwhelmed by the challenges of refugee life. I didn't want to add to their problems.

Judy and I also had little in common. She played the piano with an extraordinary talent identified by a piano-teacher neighbor not long after we moved to the housing project. Sitting at the upright mahogany Kimball at one end of our living room, she practiced Czerny finger exercises and Bach two-part inventions, gradually progressing to more advanced pieces like Chopin waltzes and Beethoven sonatas. She played the third movement of the Pathetique Sonata in C Minor in a statewide music competition in high school and won first prize. My piano lessons only resulted in frustration for both my teacher and me. As a teenager, Judy charmed boys with her pretty face dominated by almond-shaped eyes that also inspired compliments from friends and relatives. They praised me for my brains and good grades.

I sensed, and I think Judy did, too, that there was something more contributing to our lack of a sisterly bond, but we couldn't have articulated what it was. Our parents seemed oblivious to the distance between us and did little to encourage more closeness. At the same time, our mother developed an exceptionally close relationship with Judy.

A familiar scene during my preteen years: Judy and our mother huddled together on the living room sofa, at the kitchen table, on the bed in my parents' bedroom, their voices almost a whisper. Feeling left out, I'd walk up and ask, "What are you talking about?"

My mother's response was typically "You're too young to know." Judy would smirk at me. I never had a comeback. What could I do about my age? They would turn back toward each other as though I weren't there and resume their conversation. Chastened, I went to my bedroom to play or read.

They might have been gossiping about the neighbors' marital problems or discussing the facts of life, topics of no interest to me at the time. But as my mother repeated that phrase over and over to me during my childhood, I internalized it as the reason that although she seemed to enjoy *doing* things for me like sewing that splendid Hungarian costume, she preferred to spend time with my sister. Those private conversations between our mother and Judy substituted for what might have been sisterly confidences, only widening the chasm between my sister and me. And by the time I was a teenager, Judy had moved to Portland, Oregon.

* * *

I felt like an only child. With my father's help, I found solace in books—books like Thornton Burgess's *The Adventures of Chatterer the Red Squirrel,* Laura Ingalls Wilder's *Little House on the Prairie,* and Beverly Cleary's *Beezus and Ramona.* "Let's go to the library," he'd said to me in Hungarian one afternoon a few weeks after I started first grade in 1954. His blue eyes twinkled as though he had a surprise he couldn't wait to show me. I had lain awake for hours night after night in my twin bed, too excited to sleep as I thought about learning to read. The squiggles on the page that I had been trying to decipher for as long as I could remember were finally starting to make sense. I had mastered *Dick and Jane* and needed more books to challenge me. Small wonder, since my parents were both avid readers—my mother in Hungarian and my father in Hungarian and German—and they were both learning to read in English.

"Okay," I answered. Whether or not I knew what a library was, the prospect of going on an outing alone with my father enticed me. I felt special riding downtown beside him in the front seat of our Chevrolet instead of in my usual spot in the back. He held my hand and I skipped beside him as we approached the Parmly Billings Memorial Library, a turreted sandstone building on Montana Avenue a few blocks from the train station where we had arrived two years earlier. My father led me past the broad staircase leading to the main part of the library to a small door on the side at ground level. Inside, we walked down a flight of stairs to a room in a daylight basement, a cheerful, inviting space lined with shelves of books. "These are all books for children," he told me. "What do you think?"

"I love it!" I exclaimed, amazed to see so many children's books in one place.

The librarian, a rangy middle-aged woman with a tangle of gray hair pulled into a bun, approached us. Suddenly shy, I shrank close to my father. "My daughter, Erika ..." he began, struggling to find the correct words in English. He never wanted to say something unless he could get it exactly right. The librarian, hearing his accent and his hesitation, finished his sentence: "... would like a library card?"

"Yes," my father said, a smile of relief on his handsome face.

She took us to her desk and filled out a form with my name and contact information and then handed me a library card. "You can use this to check out four books for two weeks, and when you finish them, you can check out four more," she explained.

"Really?" I asked. It seemed too good to be true that I could read as many books as I wanted from this place.

The librarian led us to the shelves where books for beginning readers were located. My father watched me as I gingerly pulled one of them from the shelf and turned the pages. "Look Daddy, it's about a dog," I said, showing him one of the pictures.

"It looks interesting," he said in Hungarian. "Why don't you get it?" He waited patiently as I pulled out more books, flipped through them, put some back, set some aside. Finally, I had a pile of four. We smiled at each other as the librarian stamped each book with the due date. I hugged the books to me as we walked back to the car, my father's hand resting on my shoulder.

Still, books didn't entirely replace my longing for the companionship of another child in the family. So I was delighted when, in late 1956, my mother told me that my cousin Suzie, just two months younger than me, was coming to Billings. She and her parents, Aunt Évi and Uncle Laci, and our maternal grandparents, Nagymama and Nagypapa, had escaped from Hungary and were waiting in a refugee camp until they could join us. For the next few months, an air of celebration surrounded us as we awaited the arrival of these relatives my mother had feared she would never see again.

The reunion took place in our living room on a snowy winter day in 1957, more than two years after my first trip to the library. The space was filled to bursting, with people sitting on the sofa, my father's easy chair, the piano bench. A cacophony of voices catching up after nine years of separation mingled with the softness of Nagymama's black beaver coat against my skin as she hugged me, the cigar smell emanating from my bald Russian grandfather. Aunt Évi and Uncle Laci, thin and with bad teeth due to poor nutrition, faded into the background as I zeroed in on Suzie. "Örülök hogy itt vagy" (I'm so glad you're here), I told her before peppering her with questions about their journey. My cousin, her face pale, said little in response, watching me warily with huge brown eyes. She fingered the gold hoop set with a ruby in one of her pierced ears. None of the girls I knew wore jewelry like that, and I stared at the earring, fascinated. "Would you like to go play dolls in the bedroom?" I asked her.

"Nem" (No), she answered, burying her head in her father's shoulder. I was crushed. Still, rather than push her, I decided to back off and see what she would do on her own. She hung close to her parents, basking in their caresses and adoring looks, and answered their questions in a whiny voice.

She's a spoiled brat, I thought, even as I envied her being the object of so much affection.

My mother seemed happier with her relatives nearby and threw herself into helping them get settled in their own homes. Nagymama and Nagypapa moved into a one-bedroom duplex across the street from us, Suzie and her family into a green log house at the end of our block. My grandmother relieved Judy of caring for me and, after Aunt Évi and Uncle Laci found work, also watched my cousin. She guided and cajoled us and mediated our quarrels. Under her influence, I began to understand Suzie for the shy, scared child she was. Her parents enrolled her in Highland School, but unlike Judy, she was sent back only one grade to learn English. As we walked to and from school together and played afterward, I helped her with the language and customs that had become second nature to me after five years in Billings.

Acclimating was easier for Suzie and her parents than it had been for my family, and not only because we were there to guide them. Anti-Communist fervor still ran high three years after Senator Joseph McCarthy's hearings. With other refugees from the 1956 Revolution, our relatives were hailed as heroes who had stood up to the Communists instead of distrusted as refugees from a country on the losing side of World War II, as we had been.

Suzie joined my Brownie troop and, like the rest of us, wore our uniform of a short-sleeved light brown dress and dark brown felt beanie to our weekly meetings at Mrs. Nielson's house. One day around Thanksgiving, we were planning a skit about the Pilgrims. Each of us was to play a character named for a virtue like "faith," or "hope," words written on slips of paper that we selected from a box. Suzie drew one of the more difficult ones, "patience." Like most people learning English, she assumed that words are actually pronounced the way they're spelled. "Pā-tee-unce," she read. There was an uncomfortable pause as our fellow troop members stared at the newcomer.

"No, Suzie," I corrected her gently. "It's pā-shunts." She repeated my pronunciation with a grateful smile. I tried not to hover, but she seemed so vulnerable. I wanted to help her find the acceptance that even for me, with the veneer of Americanness I had managed to acquire, often remained elusive.

chapter eight

Secrets of a Double Life

I NAVIGATED BETWEEN my Hungarian and American worlds, trying to keep them separate, never feeling fully part of either one. There was a certain amount of comfort and safety in our Hungarian cocoon, in the familiar cadences of the language we spoke, in the traditional delicacies my mother and Aunt Évi and Nagymama prepared. Goulash and chicken *paprikás* and *pogácsa,* flaky butter biscuits, and *rétes,* strudel with apple and raisin filling, and *non plus ultra,* round Christmas cookies topped with meringue. But beyond eating and speaking Hungarian, I often felt as though I were just going through the motions. Having left Hungary as an infant, I had no personal experience of my homeland, no feelings of national pride to sustain me.

That sense of rootlessness intensified with my family's failure to talk about the important things, even among ourselves: the details of what happened in Hungary, our feelings about witnessing the murder, Robie's living in a state institution far from home, the slights and humiliations and annoyances and demands of refugee life in Billings. The lives of the

Americans around us seemed carefree in comparison, and I longed to become a full-fledged member of their world. Only by keeping my Hungarian life hidden did I believe I could ever hope to accomplish that goal. I was embarrassed whenever it was exposed, as when my parents spoke Hungarian loudly—or, worse yet, argued—in public, and people stared at us. Or when my mother and I went shopping in places like Anthony's, a discount department store in a strip mall a mile from our house.

"Ask how much this is," she whispered to me in Hungarian one day when I was nine, holding up a bath towel in the large open space with merchandise piled on display tables. Leaning toward me, she smelled of cigarettes and Blue Grass cologne.

"Do I have to?" I asked in English. Learning the language when I was four years old had enabled me to master it far more quickly and easily than my parents. But I was still shy speaking to strangers.

"Yes … I'm afraid she won't understand my accent," she said. *R*s rolled on the tongue, *z*'s or *d*'s substituting for *th* sounds, along with mispronounced words, incorrectly emphasized syllables, and faulty sentence structure did sometimes mystify Americans, though probably not to the extent my mother believed.

"Oh, all right," I said. More than her words, her eyes communicated to me just how anxious she was. Seeing my mother, so strong and capable in our Hungarian world, reduced to such self-doubt in the American one, compelled me to obey her. She handed me the towel and pushed me toward a young woman arranging merchandise on a table a few feet away.

I stood behind the clerk, shifting my weight from one foot to the other, hoping she would sense my presence. She didn't. I turned back toward my mother, my palms raised on either side of my body in a helpless gesture. She waved one arm toward me, and mouthed encouragement to do something to attract the clerk's attention. I settled for clearing my throat. The woman turned around.

"How much is this?" I stammered, my face burning.

"A dollar," she answered, giving my mother and me a long, quizzical look, a look that spoke volumes about just how far we were from being Americans.

* * *

At around the same time and closer to home, I was getting to know Nagymama during the hours she cared for me while my parents worked. One day I sat with her in the living room of her and Nagypapa's spotless duplex filled with mismatched furniture donated from various sources, snacking on buttered crusty bread she had baked. We spoke in Hungarian, since she knew only a few words of English, of the books I loved to read and the poems I was writing in Mrs. Price's third grade class. She studied me thoughtfully, her blue eyes surrounded by shadows and crow's feet. Her almost-constant smile faded. "Why doesn't Robie live at home?" she suddenly asked. I stared back at her, speechless. What could she possibly mean? Surely my parents had told her what was wrong with Robie. Surely they had explained to her and our other relatives why they had been forced to place him in a state institution far from home. But no. The bewildered look on my grandmother's face, framed by wisps of brown hair that had escaped from her bun, told me she knew none of that. I hesitated. Part of the problem was that I didn't know how to say "He's severely mentally retarded" in Hungarian, reiterating the inaccurate diagnosis of the psychologist who had evaluated him. Not that I could have said "He's autistic," either. But I was also stunned that it fell to me to deliver such a bombshell to my grandmother.

I stumbled and faltered, but finally said, "Valami baja van." (There's something wrong with him.) Nagymama no doubt guessed that much, but I was easing into the painful subject, buying time. At her blank look, I added that Robie was "*hibás*," deficient. But how to let her know in what way? I pointed to my head. "Agy," she said, citing the Hungarian word for "brain." I nodded. Finally, my grandmother put the words together, grasped their significance.

"Jaj, Istenem, a szegény gyerek" (Oh my God, the poor child), she said. Her eyes filled with tears, and she dabbed at them with a handkerchief she pulled from the pocket of the faded apron that covered the front of her body, slender except for her waist, thickening with middle age. Seeing her distress, I too started to cry. She held open her arms and we hugged, long and hard, weeping together. That moment cemented a relationship with a grandmother who became a second mother to me, comforting me and supporting me throughout my childhood.

One day, I cut my finger. As she helped me stanch the blood flowing from the wound, I asked her, "Am I going to die?"

"Of course, not! Why would you think that?"

I asked Nagymama that question often in the years after the murder. My parents no doubt mentioned to our relatives what we had witnessed, but said little more. At some point in the aftermath of that event, it had occurred to me that if the shooter's aim had been less accurate, one of us—most likely my father or me, since we were on the side of the car closest to her—might have been killed. I realized that death could strike at random, and I began to see threats of it everywhere: in rusty nails, in growling dogs, in my frequent stomachaches and bouts of strep throat. No matter how often I asked Nagymama about dying, she was always patient, always reassuring me that I would be fine. Still, without warning, a feeling sometimes swept over me, a visceral feeling that left me cold and weak, a feeling of what it means to die, to be plunged into a void and separated from the people I loved, forever. These episodes terrified me, but in my mind, they became intertwined with my parents' admonition to keep silent about what we had seen. I never told anyone about them, not even Nagymama.

At school, I blended in most of the time. But newspaper articles about the 1956 refugees had rekindled awareness of the Hungarians who had preceded them. "Hey, Erika!" yelled one of the boys as we were lining up to go back into Mrs. Price's classroom after recess. It might have been Richard, a wiry boy with tanned skin, no stranger to causing trouble. "What's the name of that country you're from again?" he asked with a malicious grin.

"Hungary," I answered in a tiny voice.

"Did you say 'Hungry'?" he jeered. "Hey, everyone, this girl's from 'Hungry'!" I hung my head as my classmates, even the girls I had just been jumping rope with, stared at me as though I were a monkey in a zoo.

"It's Hung<u>a</u>ry," I said, a little louder.

"Well, it sounds like 'Hungry' so you must be, too," he chortled. Snickers rippled through the group.

"No, I'm not," I said, jutting out my jaw. It was true that my parents were struggling to provide for us, but we always had enough to eat. Still, his message was clear—that being from Hungary was something to be ashamed of; something that made me less than the rest of them, all born in the United States.

Back in class, I slumped down in my chair and stared straight ahead, seeking solace in the smile on Mrs. Price's round, friendly face as she stood at the blackboard. I hoped that my tormentor would soon find another target, that the incident would be quickly forgotten. But there settled on me a wariness that put me constantly on guard for the next incident that would reveal I wasn't truly one of them.

And it wasn't just that I was a foreigner, or a foreigner who had witnessed a murder she couldn't talk about. I was also a foreigner who had a mentally disabled brother living in a state institution. For the first few years Robie lived at the Montana State Training School, I thought he would get better. The name of the facility implied that he would learn things, perhaps even start to talk. My best friend, Joan, whose house a block from our housing project was luxurious in comparison to ours, shared my optimism. Her short, pudgy brother, Dennis, near Robie's age, had a speech impediment and was making progress in therapy. Sitting in her bedroom filled with dolls and other toys, we planned how our brothers, mirroring us, would play together once Robie returned home. Only gradually did I realize that it was a fantasy, that Robie wasn't coming back. And in sixth grade, after my family moved and I changed schools, Joan's and my friendship ended.

* * *

That same year, Omama wrote me from her home in Austria, a letter on parchment paper covered in her spidery handwriting telling me about her life with my Aunt Marianne and Uncle Zénó and asking me about mine. My parents encouraged me to answer. I knew only the basics of written Hungarian, but my father helped me with grammar and corrected my more glaring mistakes. That first letter scrawled in pencil on pages torn from my school notebook, and the many subsequent letters I wrote during our ten-year correspondence before she died, helped me learn the accent marks used for different Hungarian vowel sounds, the correct spelling of words, the proper ways to express myself.

"Write about Robie," my father urged. He wanted me to make it seem as though my brother were fine, as though he still lived at home and shared our daily lives.

"Why?" I asked, resentful, though I knew the answer. Just as my parents hadn't told our relatives in Billings about Robie's disability, my father hadn't told his mother that her youngest grandchild was mentally disabled and had been living in a state institution for several years. He didn't tell her that because of the distance and our precarious finances, we could only visit him two or three times a year. He didn't tell her that my mother compressed months of mothering Robie into weekends spent in drab rooms at the OZ Motel on Boulder's main street; that we walked with him on unpaved side streets lined with trees and clapboard houses, holding his hands so he couldn't run away; that we picnicked with him on the banks of the shallow, rocky Boulder River, as we had in Josephine Park when he was still at home. Each time my father made his request, I tried to remember a few details from our last visit and inserted them in my letter—how Robie had grown taller, his head reaching my chin; how he had relished the pastries my mother had baked for him. I kept my comments as vague as possible, so they wouldn't stray too far from the truth. But I hated doing it.

Years later, I learned that Nagymama, who also corresponded with Omama, had passed on to her what I had told her about Robie. My paternal grandmother had known the truth all along. But she couldn't bring herself to tell my father or me that she knew. Our mutual deceit continued.

With Joan no longer part of my life, I stopped talking about Robie outside our family. I once overheard my mother tell someone she had just met that she had two daughters. No doubt she wanted to avoid addressing a painful topic with a stranger, but I took that as permission not to mention him. Keeping silent gave less ammunition to children like Billy, a towheaded, pimpled neighbor a couple of years older than me, who sneered that he'd heard I had a brother who couldn't talk. "Maybe there's something wrong with you, too," he said.

"I think my mother's calling me," I replied, a flush creeping up my neck as I turned and ran home. When anyone asked about my siblings, I told them only about Judy. But not telling people about Robie always felt wrong. Each time I denied his existence, I felt as though he were gradually being erased from our lives, like the fading of the photographs that were our only tangible reminders of him between our visits.

My deepening friendship with Suzie gave me respite. She and I rarely talked about Robie or other sensitive subjects, but by the mere fact that we both straddled Hungarian and

American worlds, we understood each other in a way that wasn't possible with others.

"Let's pretend we run a talent office in Hollywood," she suggested in English one day a couple of years after we first met. She had learned the language quickly, and that was what we spoke when it was just the two of us. We were in the living room of her and her parents' log house, lounging on cushioned bamboo chairs and leafing through her mother's movie magazines, *Photoplay* and *Modern Screen.*

"Okay," I said. Like her, I loved reading about stars like Natalie Wood and Elizabeth Taylor, whose pictures were splashed across their pages. "What shall we do?"

"We can cut out pictures of stars we like and paste them into notebooks," she said. "And then pretend we're finding them parts in movies." Suzie was always coming up with ideas like that. Earlier, she had hoped to start a local version of *The Mickey Mouse Club*, encouraged by a family friend who thought he might be able to get us on TV in connection with ads for his furniture store. We practiced songs and dances we had watched on *Mickey Mouse Club* shows aired several years after the fact in Billings. Her plan never materialized, but that didn't stop her. The fantasies she spun took us out of living in a housing project and straddling Hungarian and American worlds into carefree, sun-drenched places filled with glamour and excitement. Suzie, despite her early shyness, turned out to be the adventurous one, the risk-taker, and she took me, practical and down-to-earth, along for the ride.

* * *

A few years later, by the time Suzie and I were teenagers in the early 1960s, she would move with her parents to a newer house on the west edge of Billings; my family and my grandparents to 1920s bungalows next door to each other in a neighborhood near downtown. We would go to different schools. Our adventures would be confined mostly to the weekends.

I preferred to spend our limited time together at Suzie's, drawn by the appealing, spotless home my Aunt Évi created, with polished floors, sheets and towels folded into perfect rectangles in the linen closet, and rich, home-baked Hungarian pastries she offered guests. She doted on my cousin, but also seemed fond of me. So I was caught off guard one day in junior high when she tilted her head with its mass of unruly brown curls and studied me with cold eyes. "Why can't your father keep a job?" she demanded. As though I were responsible for my father's actions. Like my mother, Aunt Évi cleaned other people's houses for a living. But Uncle Laci didn't lose jobs the way my father did. He was skilled in watch repair, and later, fixing television sets, solitary occupations that might have suited my father better than working with others. He was also twelve years younger.

Aunt Évi's question, as Nagymama's had years earlier, stunned me. Why didn't my parents talk with our relatives about the challenges they faced? Why did *I* have to try to explain something that I hardly understood myself? My aunt's question embarrassed and hurt me." I don't know," I mumbled. What else could I say? All I knew was that my father's difficulties adjusting to a drastically diminished way of life persisted, and that my mother, hard as she worked to keep our family afloat during periods when he brought in only sporadic income from odd jobs, seemed unable to help him. Finally finding his niche as a security guard at Eastern Montana College was still in the future. After that, I avoided going to Suzie's house without my parents, unwilling to face more questions for which I had no answers. She and I would begin to drift apart, a process hastened by her family's move to Havre, 250 miles from Billings in northern Montana, when we were in high school. We'd stay in touch through occasional long phone calls and her family's visits to Billings two or three times a year.

* * *

Nagymama, just next door, compensated for Suzie's absence with support and encouragement. She ironed clothes for other people to earn money, bending her five-foot-tall body over the ironing board on her sunporch with a view of Avenue B, lined with elm trees. After school and on weekends, I sat near her and unreeled the drama of my adolescent life: my crushes on boys, my worries about my grades, my fluctuating relationships with friends and classmates, my after-school job in a doctor's office, my determination to earn a scholarship to go away to college.

"What do you think of John?" I asked her in Hungarian. She had learned English, but she was still more comfortable speaking our native language. My latest crush, a tall, slender boy with piercing blue eyes and wavy dark hair who lived nearby and came around once in a while, was one of my favorite topics.

"He's good-looking," she replied. Her reading glasses with tortoiseshell frames magnified the appreciative look in her eyes.

"Do you think he likes me?" At best, John's and my relationship was hot and cold.

"Of course, how could he not?"

Despite Nagymama's support, I felt more different than ever at school, in that adolescent pressure cooker where conformity was prized above all else. My Hungarian life was nothing like the lives of my friends. Their parents spoke without an accent, and they were less strict. Their mothers didn't work, their siblings lived at home, and their fathers watched football on TV on the weekends. They ate steak for dinner. Their houses were decorated simply, without doilies, colorful ceramics, and pictures of the Old World.

Still, some of my friends considered my Hungarian background an asset. "It's cool that you can speak another language so well," Kathy told me. Short and blonde, she was brilliant, especially in math, instead of just verging on smart and willing to study hard like I was. But we were both late bloomers struggling to find our place on the social hierarchy, somewhere between the popular girls, the cheerleaders and the majorettes, and the wallflowers, noticed by no one. I let down my guard with her, and sometimes even used my bilingual skills to my advantage.

"Why are you late?" my mother demanded when I came home from a dance with Kathy past my curfew. She was angry, but not nearly as angry as she had been on the night of my three-hour phone call with my boyfriend, Dave, when I had ignored her repeated requests to hang up. Finally, to get me to stop, she yanked the phone cord out of the wall. Her red-faced fury as she clutched the raw end of the phone cord had frightened me into compliance, but I still slipped up at times. My accomplice stood by as I explained our delay to my mother in Hungarian, foisting most of the blame onto her. Kathy knew what I was doing from the many references to her name in what she otherwise perceived as gibberish, but never held it against me. She knew she was helping me avoid punishment, freeing me for further escapades. Yet even with her, there were limits to what I was willing to share about my Hungarian life and family.

Despite my behavioral lapses, I never lost sight of my goal to go away to college. I'd heard about Macalester, a liberal arts school affiliated with the Presbyterian Church in St. Paul, Minnesota, from Dr. Johnson, one of my employers, who had earned his undergraduate degree there. Its small size of two thousand students, including many from foreign countries, and its strong financial aid program seemed like an ideal fit for me. For my first time away from home, I gravitated toward an intimate setting rather than a large university. And Macalester's emphasis on internationalism meant that my Hungarian background wouldn't seem out of the ordinary. I submitted an application, and a few months later, the college offered me admission along with a generous financial aid package to supplement my earnings and the limited financial help my parents could provide. I eagerly accepted.

The next few months passed in a blur, as I graduated from high school, worked full-time at the doctor's office, and gradually filled a black steamer trunk my parents bought me with clothes and other belongings I would take to college. My mother and Nagymama saw me off at the train station on a sunny late-August afternoon in 1966. "Örülök neked" (I'm happy for you), Nagymama said, patting my arm, but the longing in her eyes revealed how hard it was for her to see me go. I felt tears forming and rather than try to answer, put my arm around her and pulled her close. My mother was more matter-of-fact. "Study hard and don't get in trouble," she advised. Was she proud of me? My sister Judy had started college in Portland as a music major but dropped out her first year and got married. She worked at a federal agency and was the mother of a young daughter. She and my mother kept in close touch through letters, my sister's filled with stories about our parents' first grandchild. Regardless of what I would achieve in college, I knew I couldn't compete with that. Still, I longed for my mother's approval, for a closer relationship than the one we had.

I fidgeted, impatient for the Northern Pacific North Coast Limited to arrive, to distract me from the wave of homesickness and regret that suddenly threatened to engulf me. When it finally pulled into the station and we found my car, I exchanged quick hugs and kisses with my mother and grandmother before boarding.

The train carried me eastward through the plains and badlands of eastern Montana and North Dakota and the lake-filled landscapes of Minnesota, in a reversal of my family's journey fourteen years earlier. With each passing mile, thoughts of home and the people I cared about receded. I felt lighter, exhilarated, free.

PART II

Coming Into My Own

chapter nine

Breaking the Silence

MARRIAGE WAS THE last thing on my mind the March day in 1973 when I first met Leon. I was twenty-four years old, and almost three years had passed since I graduated from Macalester with a BA in psychology. As I had hoped, my college years unshackled me from the past and my Hungarian heritage. I studied hard and discovered a passion for learning about the human mind and behavior; made lifelong friends; had a few boyfriends but no real romances; experienced my share of disappointments and successes; grew up. Unsure of my next move, I stayed in Minnesota after graduation and spent the next couple of years marking time in clerical jobs and volunteering with disabled children before deciding to pursue a master's degree in social work. Longing to return to the West, I applied to several schools there, including what became my top choice, the University of Washington in Seattle.

I'd visited my sister Judy and her family there the previous Christmas and fell in love with the city set between the Cascade Range and Lake Washington to the east and Puget Sound and the Olympic Mountains to the west, with its rain and mist and gray skies, a welcome contrast to the cold, bright sharpness of Minnesota winters and the landscape's infinite flatness. At the end of my visit, Judy invited me to come live with them for an unspecified period of time. Given the tenuous nature of our relationship, I wondered whether it was a good idea. Still, I agreed to consider it. Soon after I returned to Minnesota, I received my acceptance from the University of Washington, and suddenly my sister's offer became much more appealing. I started to pack. By mid-February, I was back in Seattle, with plans to start school in the fall. I earned money in the meantime by churning out letters and memos and specifications on an IBM Selectric typewriter at a firm of demanding architects and interior designers. I had little time or energy for a social life. After college, my relationships with men had grown more serious, but none had ended well. I needed a break.

I also needed help with the myriad details involved in moving halfway across the country. My brother-in-law, Roger, suggested that I call Leon, an unmarried insurance-broker colleague of his, for help with my car insurance. I was wary. Was he trying to set me up? Still, I *did* need a local broker. "I have nothing to lose," I told myself a few days later, as I dialed Leon's number. He sounded friendly and eager to help, and he suggested that we meet for lunch near our downtown offices so I could avoid taking time off from work. On the appointed day, a slim man of medium height in wire-rimmed glasses greeted me. He had dark brown hair and a beard—unheard of among the men I had dated—and wore a polyester tweed sport coat just this side of flashy. I was underwhelmed.

"What shall I do about my car insurance?" I asked him, all

business, handing him my policy as we waited for our meals at Rosellini's 410, a popular restaurant.

He studied the coverage for my aging VW Bug. "You're getting a good deal. Stay with your current company," he advised, even though he didn't represent them. He gave me the telephone number for a competitor who did. His integrity impressed me.

Over the rest of that lunch and another a week later, I discovered that this man, eight years my senior with expressive green eyes, was different from other men I had dated. He was easy to talk to, accepting, self-confident in an unassuming way. I was smitten. But Leon already had a girlfriend. The relationship was fraying, but he felt he needed to end it before starting to see someone else. Another point in his favor. For the next few months, I put him out of my mind.

Then, in what seemed a cosmic coincidence, I ran into him in a bar after work on the very day he and his girlfriend broke up and she left for Europe. We spent several hours that evening getting reacquainted. Before long, we were dating only each other. Part of the package was his constant companion, a silver gray Siberian Husky named Ilya. Leon was helping him heal from a previous owner's physical abuse. My regard for him only grew.

Leon asked about the origin of my name, which at that time was still quite uncommon. I explained that although "Erika" is a German name, I was born in Hungary. With him, I was finally able to shed my childhood inhibitions about revealing details of my heritage to others. I told him all I knew about our escape and shared with him the challenges we had faced as refugees in Billings. He found my background interesting and maybe even a little exotic, especially my ability to speak such a unique foreign language. But for the most part, he related to me as the American woman I had become in the seven years since I had left home. I continued my longtime practice of pushing my heritage into the background except when I visited my parents in Billings. My grandparents had died within three weeks of each other the year before, and in their absence, even my childhood home seemed less Hungarian than it had once been.

As Leon's and my relationship grew more serious that fall, I knew I had to tell him about Robie. But I hesitated. Would he lose interest in me if he knew I had a brother who was autistic? Would he be upset that I had at first omitted that crucial fact, telling him only about Judy? As we cruised around Seattle in his shiny red Camaro, watched TV on the black vinyl double chaise lounge in his living room, walked Ilya in the neighborhood around his duplex apartment overlooking the Interbay railroad tracks, I rummaged through my brain for the right words to introduce the subject of my brother. They eluded me. Finally, one night when we had been dating a few months, a glass of wine at Prague, a Czech restaurant in Pioneer Square, loosened my inhibitions. Or maybe it was being in a restaurant that reminded me of my Eastern European heritage. Regardless, in dim light over a dish similar to *vadas,* the venison and dumplings my mother had cooked during my childhood, I plunged in.

"Um … there's something I've been meaning to tell you," I began.

He stroked his beard, an expectant look in his eyes. "What?" he asked. "You seem nervous."

"It's not easy for me to talk about," I said, staring at my plate.

"Is it something bad?"

"More like difficult," I said, taking a sip of wine.

"Try me," he said with a half-smile.

"I-don't-just-have-a-sister-I-also-have-a-brother-I-haven't-told-you-about," I said in a rush.

"Why is that bad?" he asked.

"There's more," I said, tears stinging my eyelids. For a moment, I couldn't speak.

"Tell me … it'll be okay," Leon said. He reached across the table and took my hand.

"He's autistic and retarded …" I began, struggling to hold back my sobs. "And he has lived in a state institution since he was six years old," I said, my voice breaking before I started crying in earnest. I grabbed my cloth napkin from the table and buried my face in it.

"I'm sorry to hear that," he said slowly. "But it doesn't change anything."

"It doesn't?" I peered out from behind the napkin.

"Why should it?"

"Because I didn't tell you the truth earlier, for one thing."

"I can understand why it was hard," he said.

"And I also wondered if you would think I have bad genes," I said, sniffling.

"Why would I be worried about your genes? Look at me. I have allergies and asthma. No one is perfect."

Was it any wonder that I loved this man? In an instant, he lifted the burden I had been lugging around for months. The rest of that evening and beyond, I told him more about Robie. I told him how we had visited him when I was a child, and how my parents still visited him as often as possible.

I poured out the feelings my brother elicited in me: guilt, regret at our lost relationship, love.

* * *

Leon and I were married less than two years later. I had just finished my MSW, and as we settled into married life, I started a job at the State of Washington Department of Social and Health Services. My career choice was no coincidence. Having grown up on society's fringes, I felt drawn toward helping others outside the mainstream: at first, mentally disabled people like Robie, and later, abused and neglected children in foster care.

The state of my genes, as well as Leon's, turned out to be irrelevant. We discovered that neither of us had a strong desire to be a parent, a qualification we deemed essential to successful child-rearing. After many discussions about the pros and cons, we decided not to have children. Instead, we poured our energies into caring for Ilya and remodeling our small mid-century modern house near Lake Washington, a badly neglected former rental Leon had bought not long after we started dating.

One June evening shortly before our second wedding anniversary in 1977, I was sitting at the counter separating the kitchen from the dining and living rooms beyond, when the phone on the wall next to me rang. It was my mother.

"We were just getting ready to visit Robie this weekend," she said, sobbing.

I stared out the window wall of the living room at the black-and-white trunks of the birch trees in the front yard with a sense of foreboding. My mother rarely cried, at least not in my presence. "What happened?"

"He died. The doctor just called us from Boulder," she said, barely able to utter the words between her sobs.

"Oh my God. How?" I asked.

"He was alone in his room after dinner. They think he threw up and choked on a string bean."

"I'm so sorry," I said, before I also burst into tears. I imagined my twenty-eight-year-old brother, my almost-twin, sitting on his dormitory bed, his thin body crumpling as he gasped for air, and no one noticing. To think that he died alone, separated from his family, with no one to comfort him, made me even sadder. So did the realization that I hadn't seen him in more than a decade. There was never time during my infrequent visits home to also make the 250-mile trek to Boulder. Instead, I relied on my mother's verbal and written updates to maintain my connection to him, and I never stopped caring.

For a few moments, my mother and I said nothing, weeping together at opposite ends of the phone line. I wondered how she would cope with Robie's death. She adored her youngest child, absent from home for more than two decades; a child who, she later pointed out to me, was the only one of her children who couldn't hurt her.

"Please keep me posted," I said before we hung up.

Leon arrived home from work and noticed my teary eyes, my smudged makeup. "What's wrong?" he asked.

"Robie died," I said. He held open his arms and I fell into them, spilling more tears on the jacket of his navy blue suit. Leon comforted me the rest of that evening. He comforted me after my mother told me about the autopsy report confirming the doctor's initial impression that my brother had regurgitated a string bean and choked on it. He comforted me after she told me that she and my father had driven to Boulder and picked up Robie's ashes, carried them home to Billings, and buried them quietly, with no service, in a plot in Mountview Cemetery overlooking the barren hills beyond the Yellowstone River, where they would eventually join him.

Later that summer, I wept at Robie's grave, marked by a small, flat granite headstone engraved, "Robert Reich, 1949–1977." Leon stood by my side.

chapter ten

Glimpse of the Past

My mother's proposal intrigued me. "Dad and I are going to visit Marianne and Zénó in Austria for two weeks in May," she told me on the phone one day in early 1978, several months after Robie's death. No doubt she and my father were seeking a distraction from their grief. "Would you and Leon like to join us?"

"It sounds like fun," I said. "Let me talk it over with him." Married three years, we wanted to travel to Europe but had yet to do so. The possibility of finally meeting my father's younger sister and her husband at their home in Eisenstadt, near Vienna, excited me, especially since I had never been able to meet Omama, who had lived with them until her death in 1971. And Eisenstadt was also just a few miles from Hungary, on the other side of the border.

I told Leon about the trip. He was also intrigued, and we discussed whether we could afford it. I was just getting started in my social work career, and we also had home remodeling expenses.

"Let's do it," he said. Like me, he had grown up in a family that struggled financially and was careful with money. Still, he spent it more easily than I did. And, he pointed out, what better way to go abroad for the first time than to visit a German-speaking country with my father, who spoke fluent German?

I called my mother back. "Count us in," I told her.

A couple of weeks later, my mother called again. "Your father and I had an argument," she said. "I'm not going to Austria after all." Then, I didn't know the details of her painful memories, memories likely to be triggered by visiting relatives linked to the time before our escape from Hungary in an area bordering our homeland. My mother had never talked about her relationship with Aunt Marianne. Perhaps my aunt had disapproved of my father's marrying a woman much younger than he was, an employee of the factory, a divorcée with a five-year-old child. Perhaps, genteel as she was, she found it difficult to relate to a sister-in-law with a fiery personality who never hesitated to speak her mind. Perhaps they hadn't gotten along, avoided each other. The prospect of staying with her and my uncle in their apartment for two weeks, an invitation my father had accepted, might have overwhelmed her. But at the time, I wasn't concerned about the impact of the trip on my mother. My own needs and desires took precedence. I wanted her to go so she and I could shop and do other things that might not interest Leon and my father.

"Please come," I begged her. "It won't be as much fun without you."

"I don't know …" she said.

"If you don't come, I'm not sure I want to go."

"I'll think about it," she said, still sounding doubtful. A few days later, she relented. "Your father and I talked again. I've decided to go."

"Wonderful!"

We talked on the phone many more times during the next three months as we finalized travel arrangements and other details. My parents joined us in Seattle for the flight to London, where we boarded another plane to Vienna. When we arrived in Austria, my mother seemed nervous, distracted, as though she didn't really want to be there. We rode the twenty-five miles from Schwechat Airport to Eisenstadt in a cab that wound through several darkened villages before depositing us in front of our relatives' multistory apartment building past midnight. The building's security system prevented us from entering the building, and we couldn't reach Aunt Marianne on the intercom. The four of us stood in the chilly dark on the sidewalk in front with our suitcases, trying to decide what to do next. Finally, Aunt Marianne, who had been watching for us, called down from her balcony. "Ti vagytok?" (Is it you?), she asked. We said it was, and she let us in, got my parents settled, and took Leon and me to the nearby Gasthof Ohr, where she had booked a room for us.

My aunt was an elegant, willowy woman with blue eyes and almost-white hair she wore in a pageboy. Her strong resemblance to my father, both in her appearance and her quiet, self-effacing manner, fascinated me. She and I weren't total strangers. We had exchanged occasional letters over the years, and, in the packages Omama sent us for Christmas, she always included a gift for me, such as a leather coin purse or a gold necklace with a pendant.

"I'm so happy you're finally here," she told me in Hungarian as she hugged me.

With two sons a decade older than I was, she seemed pleased to interact with a young female relative for a change.

"I am, too," I said.

Even though Leon and I were staying in a nearby hotel instead of with my aunt and uncle as my parents were, we spent a considerable amount of time in their home. Aunt Marianne and I hit it off from the start. And being with her where Omama had also lived for many years made me feel a tie to my deceased grandmother.

Uncle Zénó was an affable, balding man with a ready smile and a slightly irreverent sense of humor. He and my aunt were gracious hosts in their comfortable apartment with oil paintings decorating the walls, oriental rugs covering the hardwood floors, and panoramic views from large windows of flat farmland bordered by windbreaks south of town.

Aunt Marianne was interested in Leon's and my lives. "Tell me about your jobs," she urged a few days into our visit. We had joined her and my parents from the Gasthof Ohr for a walk in the park near their home. When my Hungarian vocabulary failed me in explaining child welfare social work and insurance, my parents stepped in to help. Leon, of course, understood nothing, and I translated for him. At times, the conversation between my parents and relatives was about people I had never met and events that had occurred long ago, topics that no doubt would have captured my interest once I began to explore my heritage, but that was still twenty-five years in the future.

As it was, I paid scant attention and understood little. Still, we enjoyed getting acquainted, both in their home and as we toured the charming town with its Baroque buildings, including the former home of the composer Joseph Haydn and the imposing but faded Eszterházy Palace, the former seat of the powerful aristocratic landowners of the pre-WWI

Austro-Hungarian Empire. I had no way of knowing that this would be our only meeting, that my aunt and uncle would die within months of each other just three years later. I anticipated more visits, more time to deepen a relationship that had started on such a positive note.

Things did not go well with my mother, and I wasn't sure why. Did she resent me for talking her into going to Austria? Did my presence magnify her negative reactions to an emotionally charged situation, since I was the child born to her amid the turmoil before our escape? She didn't say. In our family, we never addressed concerns head-on. Regardless, she seemed annoyed with me on an excursion to Vienna early in the trip. My aunt and uncle stayed home, leaving the four of us to sightsee on our own. We strolled the pedestrians-only Kärtnerstrasse, the main shopping street; admired the geometric-designed roof and spires of the Stephansdom, Vienna's landmark church; toured the Burggarten, a city park with white swans floating on a lake and a statue of Mozart, my favorite composer. But after lunch at a tavern, my mother and I disagreed about how to see more of the city.

"We need to go on a bus tour," she said.

"I'd like to walk more," I said. The spring day was balmy, and our Michelin guide provided information about other sights near the center that we could see on foot. We set out, but Leon and I had trouble interpreting some of the maps and directions.

"This is a waste of time," my mother said. "Let's take the bus tour."

"Why don't you and Dad go on the tour, and we can meet up later at the bus station to go back to Eisenstadt?" I asked. Oblivious to the toll the trip must have been taking on my mother, I saw my suggestion as a reasonable way to resolve our impasse. Later, I would see that perhaps my parents were tired of walking. It would have been so easy for me to go along with my mother's wishes. But stubbornness, coupled with a desire to have my own way that I had discovered since my marriage, prevented me from doing so. My mother's icy demeanor toward me on the bus ride back to Eisenstadt told me the price I had paid.

Still, Leon and I took another side trip with my parents a few days later, to Pinkafeld, an hour or so away, where Omama was buried in the Friedrich family crypt. Leon drove our rental car up and down the town's hilly streets as my father tried to recall the location of the cemetery. "It might be over that way," he said, pointing southward on a street paralleling the highway that had brought us to town. But it wasn't. "Or maybe it's on the far side of the highway." We headed up the hill in that direction.

No doubt my mother's tension had been building up in her, and outside our relatives' scrutiny, she felt free to unleash it.

"Why don't you know where it is?" she demanded in a shrill voice, though the last time my father had been in Pinkafeld was on a visit to Austria twenty years earlier. Her berating him bothered me as much as it had when I was a child. Still, wanting to avoid antagonizing her further, I said nothing. Leon and I hunkered down in the front seat, trying to be invisible.

My mother eventually calmed down and we paid our respects at Omama's grave. Afterward, we tracked down a family acquaintance Marianne had told us about.

"Are there any roofers in town who lived here in 1948?" my mother asked her.

"One," she said. "Willi." She gave us directions to his house, and we found him there, a stout, balding, middle-aged man.

"I escaped from Hungary in 1948 and you helped me get past the Soviets on the bus from Oberwart to here," my mother told him in Hungarian.

"That was a long time ago," Willi responded, ducking his head. He seemed embarrassed, or perhaps reluctant to remember.

My mother pushed me forward. "This is the baby I was carrying in my arms," she said. "Look how she's grown up." Willi and I exchanged bashful smiles. Long before I began to delve into my family's past, I failed to appreciate the significance of meeting the man who had saved my mother and me from being sent back to the ÁVO, the Secret Police, in Hungary. If I had, I would have inundated him with questions. Was he working for someone who helped escapees, or was it truly a chance meeting between him and my mother? Why was he willing to take the risk? What would have happened to him if he had been caught? Did he help others? And, most important, I would have thanked him profusely for enabling me to live my entire life in freedom.

Despite such bright spots, my mother was still angry with me about our disagreement in Vienna. There was no mistaking how she moved away from me, muttered sarcastic asides to my comments, avoided eye contact. Rather than risk further confrontations, Leon and I decided to take some side trips on our own.

One was to the area around Neusiedler See, a large, shallow lake straddling the border between Austria and Hungary. We emerged from our rental car on a warm, sunny morning at the end of the road outside the village of Mörbisch. A sign with the words "Achtung! Staatgrenze" announced in German that we had arrived at the border. Verdant plains dotted with deciduous trees and the distant, glinting surface of the lake extended southeastward into Hungary. My first glimpse of my homeland. Before us was a knee-high, red-and-white gate-arm barrier. We could easily have stepped over it. But several yards beyond, two tall, parallel barbed-wire fences, perhaps ten or twelve feet apart, their tops angled inward, stretched in either direction toward the horizon. Watchtowers topped with small enclosures rose at intervals next to them on the Hungarian side. On the tower closest to us, within shouting distance, a guard flanked by a German Shepherd strolled back and forth gripping a rifle. The Iron Curtain. When I'd heard that term as a child, I had imagined actual draperies constructed of iron, red like the Soviet flag, though I could never figure out how they were hung. The reality was more mundane, though the wires on top of the fences were no doubt electrified, and mines were buried in the soil around them. Millions of Hungarians, including some remaining relatives and family friends, were imprisoned behind that border. A chilling thought. If we hadn't escaped, we would have been among them.

Going into Hungary that day, even for a brief visit, was out of the question, and not only because we lacked the requisite visas. My family had escaped the country as "class aliens," and my parents worried that if any of us were to return, the Communists might detain us, perhaps permanently. Still, I was curious to see more. Later in the day, after paddleboating on the lake, we drove a few miles south to the border crossing at Klingenbach. Next to an ocher building that was the Austrian checkpoint—there would have been a Hungarian one farther on—a more formidable gate-arm barrier blocked the road. We could see little beyond it in the deepening dusk, but at least could tell that there were official ways to get into and out of Hungary for visitors, if not for most residents. I stepped out of the car to take a photograph, and an Austrian guard rushed from the building. "Verboten," he said in German, pointing to the camera. But he didn't confiscate my film.

Leon eased the car back in the direction we had come. "Stop," I said after we had gone several yards. Leaning out of the window, I snapped a picture. A small act of defiance against minefields, watchtowers, and barbed-wire fences.

chapter eleven

Revelation

A COUPLE OF weeks after we returned from Austria, I received a phone call from Judy. She sounded agitated, breathless, not at all like the calm, unruffled sister I knew. "You'll never guess what Mom told me while she and Dad were here," she said.

"What?" I asked.

"Dad isn't my biological father," Judy said.

It took a moment for her words to sink in. I was stunned. Speechless. At thirty-five and thirty, Judy and I had lived our entire lives assuming that we both carried the genes of the father who raised us. But we had sensed at times during our childhood that our parents weren't telling us the whole story. They never talked about Judy's birth. They never compared her to our father or encouraged her to write to his relatives as they did me. And her remarkable musical talent seemed to have no source in a family that was decidedly unmusical.

"Are you there?"

"Uh … yeah," I finally answered. "Are you serious?"

"Would I make something like that up?"

"How did you find out?" I asked. Following our trip, my parents had picked up their car in Seattle and driven to Portland to visit Judy and her family before returning to Montana.

"Mom and I stayed up late drinking wine one night, and I got up the nerve to ask her for my birth certificate." Our mother had always been evasive with her about that document, and Judy had wondered why. "I told her I want to get a passport so I can go to Europe, too."

"What did she say?"

"She told me she'd been married before, to a man named János Oroszlán in Vasvár. He's my biological father."

"Wow!" I exclaimed. Despite Judy's and my suspecting that our parents had withheld information from us, I, at least, hadn't anticipated anything of this magnitude. With our mother's revelation, the picture we'd had of our family all these years was torn to shreds.

"Did Mom say anything about him, what he was like?" I asked.

"He was a gifted musician, a bandleader." Finally, the answer to my frustrated piano teacher's question about why I couldn't play like Judy.

"What else?"

"She said he was a liar."

I wondered what Judy's birth father had done to warrant such a harsh assessment by our mother.

"But beyond telling me his last name, she refused to say anything more after that. She went to bed and didn't get up for a couple of days."

"It must have been hard for her to tell you after all this time," I said. Working in the field of child welfare, I knew how challenging it could be for adoptive parents to reveal to their children that they were adopted and had birth parents.

Even though this situation only involved Judy's father, it was similar. And it was always more difficult if parents waited instead of telling children when they were young, enabling them to grow up with the knowledge as a natural part of their lives. No doubt the stress of finally revealing the truth to Judy overwhelmed our mother, who tended to cope with negative feelings by going to bed.

"Yes, but *I* could have used some comforting after such a huge shock. As it was, Dad asked me to go to her and make her feel better," she said in an aggrieved tone.

"I'm not surprised." Our mother's feelings typically took precedence in our family. The rest of us tiptoed around her to try to keep the peace, though my father and Judy were more adept at it than I was. Outspoken like her, I often said what I thought, setting off conflicts like the one in Austria.

"By the way, Mom and Dad made me promise not to tell you," Judy said.

Then why did you? I thought. Unlike me, Judy would never have tried to convince my parents to change their minds. But afterward, she must have decided that since she knew, I should, also. And she obviously needed to talk to someone who had shared her experience living in our family, someone who would understand.

"So what does that mean, exactly?"

"You can't tell them that I told you."

"Wait, after all this time, Mom has told you about your father, and now I have to pretend that I don't know?" I asked, incredulous.

"They were worried that if you knew, you would treat me differently."

I was furious that my parents didn't give me more credit.

My father might have, but this was my mother's secret, her decision to make. And I was angry at Judy for putting me in this position. But then I wondered, *Did* knowing the truth make a difference to me? Judy's and my relationship had always been shaky. Would knowing she had a different father push us further apart? Or would the knowledge that our parents and relatives had deceived us both for all these years pull us together? I wasn't sure. But I couldn't help empathizing with my sister. It must have been frustrating for her to finally learn about her birth father, only to be denied information about him that she had every right to know.

"Okay, I won't tell," I promised.

And I didn't—for the next eight years.

* * *

Soon after Judy and I talked, my father quietly filed papers to adopt her. Now that Judy finally knew the truth, our parents no doubt wanted to ensure that she had the same rights as I did. Added protection in case I found out and *did* treat her differently. Despite my shock and anger, part of me understood why my mother, upset as she was after telling Judy, hadn't wanted to involve me. "How could you lie to us for all those years?" I would have demanded. And I would have asked more questions about János, pushed her to reveal more than she had to Judy. We would have gotten into a major argument.

I deeply regretted my role in the discord between my mother and me in Austria. When my parents had picked their car up at our house before driving to Portland, she had spoken to me in clipped sentences and wouldn't look at me.

In the ledger she seemed to keep of my actions, the negatives yet again outweighed the positives. I wanted to apologize, to resolve our differences. But I knew better than to try. My mother never made up until she was ready. My anger at her lack of trust in me, coupled with her anger over the trip, created more friction than usual between us. Still, our letters, phone calls and annual visits continued, though perhaps on a more superficial level than usual.

"I think I should tell Mom I know," I said to Judy every once in a while in the years after she told me.

"No, don't! You'll get me in trouble," she would reply, sounding more like a frightened child than a woman approaching forty. She seemed to have little concern for how *I* felt, how keeping the secret was gnawing away at me, consuming more and more of my energy. Sometimes, she even fueled the fire. "Mom thinks you and Leon took off on your own in Austria because he leads you around by the nose," she said, not long after we learned the secret.

"That's ridiculous," I told her. When Leon and I got married, we had omitted from our vows the promise that I would obey him because we both viewed our relationship as one of equals.

"I know," she answered. But the damage was done.

That was the first of many negative messages Judy passed on to me from our mother. At first, even though it hurt, I was curious about my mother's true feelings behind the civil façade she presented to me. But three or four years after we learned about János, I'd had enough. "I don't want to know what Mom says about me anymore," I told her. "If you try to tell me, I'm not going to listen." Setting that boundary marked a turning point. I could begin to imagine reconciling with our mother, though doing so would take several more years.

I resented Judy's role in the conflict. Still, perhaps wanting to prove to my parents that I wouldn't treat her differently, I continued to reach out, trying to get closer to her and to be a loving, attentive aunt to my niece and nephew.

Finally, I knew I needed to also reach out to my mother. Anger seemed to energize her, but it had always depleted me. In 1986, I wrote her a letter offering to resolve our differences.

"Call me," she wrote back. "Our conversation won't be unpleasant."

"I know about Judy's father," I said. "She told me not to tell you and keeping quiet about it has been really hard for me all these years."

"You should have told us you knew right away," my mother said, far calmer than I had anticipated.

"Wouldn't you have been upset?"

"No." But eight years had passed since she had taken to her bed after telling Judy. The reality back then would no doubt have been different.

A truce. The tension between my mother and me abated. Judy continued to be curious about her father, but he was still a forbidden subject as far as our mother was concerned. Aunt Évi and Uncle Laci might have filled in the blanks, but they had cooperated in keeping the secret. Where would their loyalties lie if we started to ask them questions about János?

* * *

During the next few years, as we assimilated the reality of Judy's birth father, the urgency to know more receded. But in the early 1990s, more than a decade after my mother revealed her secret to Judy, I met a woman through work who had started an organization to help birth parents and adoptees find each other.

"Shall I ask her if she can track down János?" I asked Judy.

"Sure, why not?" she said.

Within days, we had his address in Vasvár. Judy drafted a letter to him in English, explaining that she hadn't even known he existed until she was thirty-five, and had only recently discovered how to contact him. She said she wanted to become acquainted with him, to get answers to a lifetime of questions. My long correspondence with Omama had made me more fluent in the written language than Judy was, and I translated her letter into Hungarian. A few weeks after she mailed it, she received a response from her birth father. He sounded like a romantic, describing himself at work in his garden, gazing wistfully at jets flying far overhead and imagining her on board, coming to see him. Judy and I were both charmed.

Neither of us told our mother about finding János, about the exchange of letters, until many years later. Not doing so felt wrong, but given her refusal to talk about him, we felt we had no choice. By then, I was the director of an adoption program and felt more convinced than ever of Judy's right to know her birth father, to learn as much as she could from him while there was still time. He was already in his early seventies. Judy and he exchanged more letters and photos, too—of János as a blond, handsome young man and an aging one, his girth increased, his hair nearly gone; of Judy and

Roger and my teenage niece and nephew on the deck of a beach house at sunset.

But as the relationship grew, an obstacle arose. "My wife can't know about our correspondence," János said in a letter. She would be upset to learn that he was in touch with his child from his former marriage. He suggested that Judy send her letters to his daughter, her half sister, in Szombathely instead. He hoped that if Judy ever traveled to Hungary, they could meet at his family's cabin at Lake Balaton, a safe fifty miles from Vasvár.

"There have been too many secrets already," Judy shot back. "I refuse to be a secret now." János never responded.

I wondered how Judy could start a relationship with her birth father, only to let it go as easily as she did. Given how long he had been a secret in our family, it made sense that she didn't want to be a secret in his. But I wanted them to find common ground. For her, no doubt, it was more than just the secrecy. After so much time, the prospect of incorporating into her life this man whose genes comprised half of who she was might have proved too intense, too complicated. What would he want from her? What could she give? Still, I couldn't have imagined letting him go if I were in her position. But Judy and I are different. I'm more emotional and sentimental than she is. I work and work and work on relationships even when they seem impossible. Even as she backed away, the mystique of a birth father she never fully knew continued to capture my imagination.

chapter twelve

Cultural Awakening

I SAT IN a darkened theater in 2004, engrossed in a Hungarian movie about two men, a father and son. In one scene, they stand on a rise in a field of dry weeds, gazing out over a landscape of verdant hills under brooding clouds. The father is middle-aged, his face rugged, one eye milky, sightless, an ex-convict returned home after a long imprisonment. The son, in his early twenties, has restless dark eyes and high cheekbones, his muscular body taut with hatred for his father, whose absence he blames for his mother's death. The taciturn father has no words to bridge the divide. Complicating their relationship is the mother's younger sister, a raven-haired beauty who has joined the household to help the father and son. She becomes the father's lover, but the son also has a crush on her. The men battle over the vineyard the father is determined to carve out of the land with the help of his reluctant son, and the son's drifting toward a life of crime the father is determined to leave behind. In the end, neither wins.

The movie, filmed in the wine country near Gyöngyös, a town ninety miles east of Budapest, was part of the Seattle International Film Festival, which typically screened a couple of offerings from Hungary each year. My father's 2003 letter to me had sparked interest not only in my family's history but in all things Hungarian, including these windows into the culture of my homeland. I liked listening to actors speaking my native language and using familiar idioms and expressions, like the black-clad grandmother in one movie, who, not unlike my own Nagymama, wailed "Szörnyű" (dreadful), when anything bad happened. The actors often spoke rapidly, but I understood most of the dialogue and only occasionally needed to refer to the English subtitles.

Images and characters from the movies, with often-melancholy themes, stayed with me long after the closing credits: people hiding from the authorities in a field of waving wheat, a woman cleaning toilets in a Budapest subway station, a young girl abandoned by her parents and kidnapped into sex slavery. One movie, filmed in black-and-white, consisted of a series of surreal scenes in rural settings among falling leaves—the funeral of a child in a white casket, men breaking horses in a corral. I tend to think linearly and struggled to connect the scenes into a coherent narrative. Only later did I realize that the movie, of the fabulist genre, was not intended to be a story, but was deliberately fragmented, ambiguous, filled with unanswered questions, not unlike my understanding of my family's history before I began my quest.

My renewed interest in my roots prompted me to start speaking Hungarian with my parents more than I had in many years, and I discovered serious gaps in my vocabulary. I bought *NTC's Hungarian & English Dictionary*, billed as the most up-to-date reference available, to supplement a couple of pocket-sized dictionaries I already owned. Poring over it, I found many words unfamiliar to me. Words like "*ábrándozni*"(ah-brawn-doze-ni), meaning "to daydream," and "*aggódalom*"(aw-go-doll-om), meaning "anxiety" and ó*vó**hely*"(o-vo-high), meaning "refuge." I printed the words and their definitions on opposite sides of fluorescent pink, orange, yellow, and green index cards and kept them in a rubber-banded pile on my desk. Every day or two I would flip through the cards, testing myself on the meaning of the words. Sometimes I knew that "*bizalom*"(bee-za-loam) meant "trust," or that "*méltóság*" (male-toe-shog) meant "dignity," and sometimes I didn't. But gradually, the correct meaning of the words began to stay with me. At the same time, I reveled in the unique cadences of the words, in the poetry of my native language. I began to see how, by its very nature, Hungarian encouraged the hyperbole my Aunt Évi, especially, was prone to use, as when she described a floral gift as the most gorgeous bouquet of flowers she had ever seen, or her granddaughter's classmates as so envious of her new necklace that they almost ripped it from her neck.

In 2004, I became a volunteer docent at the Seattle Public Library's new Rem Koolhas-designed, glass-and-metal headquarters downtown and was delighted to discover that the foreign language collection included several shelves of Hungarian books. Before or after my tours, I'd thumb through them, searching for volumes with lots of white space on the page for easier reading. I checked out poetry and short story collections, and, sometimes, a children's fairy tale with its simpler vocabulary. I was relatively proficient speaking and writing Hungarian, but reading remained a challenge. At my desk or in bed before going to sleep at night, I plodded through the books, my trusted dictionary at my side.

Sometimes unfamiliar words weren't listed, and I was forced to discern the meaning from the context.

Once, to experience a narrative as I did in English, without fits and starts, I translated a short story, "The Lousy Thousand," by Susan Vathy. Set during the Communist era, it is about Valika, a woman with two sons and a crumbling marriage, who wakes up one day with a headache. She goes to her job as a secretary in a government office to find that her bosses are absent. Instead of doing the typing that has piled up on her desk, she chats with a co-worker about her family problems. Later, she daydreams about her upcoming vacation, perhaps among the vineyards where her mother-in-law lives, and about trying to patch things up with her husband. She decides to surprise him with a phone call at work, but the line is busy. Looking around the office, she notices the dirty cups of her superiors on top of the refrigerator. She is tired of their ignoring her complaints that cleaning up after them isn't part of her job description and decides to take action. She takes cups from the cupboard and labels them with her bosses' names to force them to assume responsibility for their own messes. Taking charge gives her a brief surge of optimism, and she notices her headache is gone. She forgets about the call to her husband. Instead, she hurries to lunch, to avoid ending up with "the dregs of everything." The largely pessimistic worldview of the story, like that of the movies, pervaded many of the books I read. Was it the result of the years Hungary spent under Communist rule, or something more entrenched in the culture?

* * *

For as long as I could remember, my parents displayed paintings and colorful ceramics and other art objects from Hungary. In our own home, Leon and I preferred Asian art and etchings in muted colors and shelves uncluttered with objects that required dusting. But during a visit to Billings a couple of years after my father's letter, I was chatting with my mother at the dining room table when I noticed the porcelain figures of a Hungarian peasant man and woman in the glass-fronted credenza next to us. They had been part of my parents' collection since the 1960s. "May I take them out?" I asked my mother.

"Of course," she said.

I lifted them gingerly from their resting place near the china cups and saucers my mother also collected and placed them on the table. The man was about nine inches tall, his face dominated by a brown mustache that curled up at the ends. In his mouth was a long, curved pipe. He wore a black sheepskin Cossack hat and a *szűr*, a full-length white felt cape that I later learned was from the Bugac region of eastern Hungary, edged in black sheepskin and decorated with leaves and flowers in primary colors. The woman, slightly shorter, wore an orange kerchief and a waist-length version of the man's cape, a long orange skirt, and a large apron with a row of floral designs near the hem.

"They're beautiful," I said to my mother, as though seeing them for the first time. I caressed the woman's figure with its slight sheen. "So simple." I had seen larger, more ornate figurines of Hungarian peasants, but given my "less is more" approach to decorating and just about everything else, I found these far more appealing.

"Do you want them?" my mother asked me with a smile, nudging the figures toward me.

I hesitated. The pieces would be a wonderful symbol of my awakened interest in my Hungarian heritage. "No," I finally said. "I know how much you like them and would hate to take them from you."

She didn't protest.

On my birthday a few months later, I opened a package from my parents to find a gift-wrapped box. Inside were the two figurines. Tears sprang to my eyes at my mother's thoughtful, generous gesture. But I was dismayed to see that, in transit, the female figure had broken into three pieces: her head and shoulders, her torso, and her skirt. I later placed the man in a prominent spot on a shelf in the family room. Until I could figure out what to do with her, I scooped the pieces of the woman up from the coffee table to store them in a more secure place next to him. Balancing them in my hands, I turned toward the shelf. Suddenly, the pieces slipped from my grasp onto the floor and shattered. "Oh no!" I exclaimed, momentarily frozen, before I knelt down to pick up the pieces. All thirteen of them.

"Thanks so much for the figurines," I told my parents on the phone afterward.

"Do you like them?" my mother asked.

"Oh, yes," I said. I didn't mention the original damage to the female figure or the more grievous damage I had inflicted on her. Why ruin my mother's joy at giving me such a perfect gift? I would fix this damage. It wasn't just the sentimental value of the piece. The broken figurine seemed to represent all that had gone wrong for my family since the takeover of the factory, the Reich Gépgyár, in Hungary in

1948. I couldn't repair my parents' shattered dreams or the disappointments of refugee life in Billings. But a replaced or restored figurine *could* inspire me as I tried to pull together the missing fragments of my own life. Immersing myself in Hungarian culture was a start. Still, to fully achieve my goal, I knew I needed to return to my homeland.

I tried to find an identical figurine. I spent hours at my computer, searching countless websites of porcelain dealers and found figures that were taller or shorter, more colorful or plainer, more serious or more whimsical. But none that matched mine. Repairing her seemed to be the only answer. Fortunately, I had saved not only the thirteen main pieces, but every single shard and sliver I could sweep from the floor. My search shifted from dealers to firms that repaired porcelain, and I found several. The one that most impressed me was a company in Beverly Hills, California. Their website showed "before" photographs of shattered vases and other objects, some in even more pieces than my figurine. In almost unbelievable "after" pictures, the objects were fully restored, with no sign that they had ever been broken. I called the firm and told the woman who answered about my fractured figurine. "How much would it cost to fix it?" I asked.

"Send us some photographs," she said. "That's the only way I can give you a firm estimate."

I put the pieces on a dark cloth, photographed them from several angles, and mailed the pictures to the firm. After they arrived, the woman called me.

"If you want the pieces put back together and don't mind if the cracks show, it would cost $250," she said.

"I want it to look like the photographs on your website," I said.

"That would cost $725." I gasped. The amount was much higher than I had expected, certainly far more than the dollar value of the piece.

"I'll get back to you," I told her. I talked it over with Leon, weighing the pros and cons of spending so much money. But I soon decided to go ahead. The figurines were intended to be a pair, and I longed to display them in their original beauty, both as inspiration to me and as a public statement of my efforts to retrieve my Hungarian heritage from the shadows.

The firm gave me detailed shipping instructions, and I spent an entire evening taping bubble wrap around each individual piece before nesting them all in an oversized box filled with Styrofoam peanuts. I enclosed the required 50 percent deposit, and the next day, mailed the box to California.

When the company called me a couple of months later to inform me that the work was complete, I sent a check for the balance. A smaller box soon arrived in the mail. Inside was the Hungarian peasant woman. I lifted her out of the box and examined her from every angle. Her shattered fragments had been formed back into a perfect whole.

Within a few months, Leon and I were on our way to Hungary.

PART III

Going Back

chapter thirteen

First Encounter: Budapest

THE CLOUDS THAT blanketed Europe on our flight from Amsterdam on a late-September day in 2006 dispersed as we approached Budapest, revealing the Danube River far below, gleaming silver in sunny autumn haze. A good omen. Our Malev Hungarian Airlines Boeing 737 descended over suburbs of tidy, red-roofed stucco houses nestled among green trees before making a steep turn and landing at Ferihegy Airport ten miles southeast of the city. I was giddy with excitement and almost danced out of the plane behind Leon. Fifty-eight years after leaving Hungary in my escaping mother's arms, I was finally back in my homeland.

I'm the one who plans our trips, makes the reservations, and studies the guidebooks. I always want things to go as smoothly as possible, but this time it was more important to me than ever before. As we strolled on the polished marble floors of the modern terminal to claim our bags, I fantasized that the first Hungarians I encountered would recognize me as their compatriot, returned at long last; that they would sense the significance of this trip to me. Of course, no one did. Not the blond young man in the blue uniform at Passport Control who barely glanced at Leon's passport but silently scrutinized mine for so long that I squirmed (was it because I was born in Hungary?); not the quartet of customs officers who ignored us at the green door for travelers with nothing to declare; not the clerk at the information desk who politely informed us it would be a forty-five-minute wait for the next shuttle into the city; not the two strapping men half-heartedly digging a trench near the sidewalk where we waited for a cab I had called on the advice of our guidebook to avoid taking an overpriced airport taxi.

Despite the cool reception, I was pleased that we would be spending the first week of our two-week trip in this cosmopolitan city of 1.8 million, sometimes dubbed "the Paris of the East." Budapest would enable me, like a bather easing into one of the city's many steaming thermal baths, to acclimate to Hungary gradually, without the emotional turmoil I suspected awaited me in Szombathely and Vasvár, towns a hundred miles to the west in Vas Megye (Iron County), at the heart of my family's history. My father had visited Budapest with his family as a child, and he and my mother had traveled there as newlyweds. He had tried in vain to find a job there after the Communists seized the factory. But my family had no real ties to the city, viewing it mostly from afar as the center of national culture and politics.

"It doesn't look like our cab is coming," Leon said after we spent a half hour watching numerous taxis race by us on the airport drive.

"No kidding," I replied. "Maybe the dispatcher didn't understand me when I told her where we would be waiting." I had no experience conducting business on the telephone in Hungarian and may also have misunderstood her instructions to me.

"I don't want to wait anymore," Leon said. "Let's take an airport cab."

"Oh, all right," I agreed. I tend to follow the advice of guidebooks to the letter on overseas trips, but we hadn't slept in twenty-four hours. The sooner we could get to our hotel and relax, the better.

The line for airport cabs wasn't long, and a paunchy, middle-aged driver soon waved us over. "Jó napot" (Good day), I said to him after we were settled in his compact car, hoping to dispel any notion that we were naïve American tourists. He responded with the more formal "Kezét csókolom" (I kiss your hand), then fell silent as he drove away from the airport, apparently finding idle chitchat incompatible with driving at breakneck speed, zigzagging between lanes, and riding the bumper of the car ahead of us. Leon and I swayed from side to side in the back seat, my hair blowing in my face from the draft coming in the driver's open window. I stole a glance at my gray-bearded spouse. His half-smile tried to reassure me, but I clutched his hand in a viselike grip. Whizzing by our window were miles of railroad tracks, dreary industrial areas, and drab Communist-era apartment buildings defaced with graffiti.

The scene changed as we approached downtown Pest, the city's government, financial, and commercial center. Ornate buildings in Classicist, Romanesque, Gothic, and Art Nouveau styles began to appear along the street. My spirits lifted, and I soon felt as elated as I had seeing the centers of other European cities we had visited, including London, Vienna, Munich, and Milan, a sense of kinship with the Old

World of my origins. Still, I was dismayed to see black scribbles of graffiti marring even some of those venerable structures. The narrow, winding streets forced our driver to slow down, but he still darted perilously among cars and bicycles before racing across the sleek white metal Elizabeth Bridge over the Danube to the city's other half, historic Buda on the west bank.

A mile or so north on the Bem rakpart, the tree-lined boulevard overlooking the river, he slammed to a stop in front of the Hotel Victoria. I leaped from the car, Leon close behind me. "That was one scary ride!" I exclaimed in English, unable, in the heat of the moment, to summon the necessary words in Hungarian. The driver gave no indication whether he understood, and he probably didn't, because he handed me a business card and invited me to contact him for the return trip. I slipped it into my pocket and crumpled it.

We pushed open the glass-paned door of the twenty-seven-room hotel, a narrow, unpretentious building abutting its neighbors in the middle of the block. "Hello, hello," the desk clerk greeted us in English. "I'm Gaby." She got up from behind the desk, a lithe woman clad in a chic black pantsuit, and helped us haul our suitcases up several stairs to the compact lobby. "Welcome to Budapest," she said, a smile on her freckled face. "We're so glad you're here."

Her friendly, disarming manner dispelled my concerns about my failed conversation with the taxi dispatcher and inspired me to utter more than the few other phrases I had spoken since our arrival. I'd held back not only because of my incomplete vocabulary, but also my accent. Since I'd grown up speaking Hungarian, I didn't have an American accent, but I *did* speak with an accent unique to Vas Megye. It's all in how the letter "e" is pronounced. In Budapest, the sound is similar in most cases to that in the English word, "let." In Vas Megye, "e" can also be pronounced like the vowels in "fur" or "raw" or "lie." If you speak with a non-Budapest accent, some Hungarians view you with disdain, as though you're too ignorant to speak the language correctly. Disdain or ridicule was the usual reaction I elicited when speaking my native language with Hungarians I met as an adult in the United States.

"Isn't she cute, the way she tries to speak Hungarian?" asked a Hungarian artist of local renown whom I had just met at a party given by one of Leon's business partners a few years after we were married. She didn't really expect an answer from the people standing around us, but her meaning was clear. And when, a couple of years later, I told a Hungarian tailor marking a suit Leon had bought for alterations that I was born in Szombathely, he responded by correcting my pronunciation. Encounters like these humiliated me, and my confidence plummeted. I avoided speaking Hungarian outside my family and hadn't done so for years. But if Gaby harbored any critical thoughts, she gave no sign, perhaps because her English was also not flawless. In the warmth of her accepting attitude, speaking Hungarian felt safe again. I had the sudden urge to speak it with everyone I encountered—the hotel handyman, the chambermaid, the manager—to begin my transformation from an American tourist to someone who might be able to pass as a native.

Leon and I settled into our simple but comfortable eighth-floor room, delighted with its panoramic view of the Danube and the far, flat reaches of Pest beyond. The stately neo-Gothic Parliament building stood on the far bank of the river to the north; to the south, the graceful Széchenyi Lánchid (Chain Bridge) stretched across it. We were tired, but decided against taking a nap after I recalled that the effects of jet lag can be relieved by staying awake until the local bedtime. Instead, we went downstairs and asked Gaby about restaurants where we could have an early dinner. She recommended the Horgásztanya (Fisherman's Farm), a nearby bistro, and we strolled there on the sidewalks of Watertown, a pleasant district of shops, restaurants, and apartments, once home to artisans and fishermen, in the shadow of Castle Hill, a popular tourist destination.

Sunlight filtered through locust, linden, and ash trees with green leaves just beginning to turn gold in late September. Posters with large colored portraits of candidates in local elections hung from light standards overhead. A streetcar crammed with passengers clanged past on tracks near the sidewalk. Beyond them, a steady stream of honking cars moved on the wide boulevard. The acrid smell of exhaust fumes mingled with fleeting odors of fresh-baked bread, rotting garbage, roasting meat. On the buildings, more graffiti. I drank in the sights and sounds and smells with the same awe I feel in any new place I visit, but with an added sense that, on some elemental level I had yet to discern, Budapest was somehow connected to me.

At the restaurant, Leon and I sat outdoors on wooden benches at a table covered with a red-and-white checked tablecloth, separated by a railing from a street clogged with cars. A swarthy waiter in a white apron brought us glasses of pinot gris from the Badacsony area of Lake Balaton to start our meal.

"To my finally being back in Hungary," I said, clinking my glass with Leon's.

"To your finally being back in Hungary," he repeated, smiling. He, more than anyone, knew just how much time and effort I had spent to arrive at this milestone.

We dined on chicken *paprikás* and *nokedli*, pearly oval Hungarian noodles. It felt surreal to be savoring the tender morsels of chicken and tasty noodles smothered in a rich sauce of sour cream and paprika not at my parents' lace-covered dining room table in Billings, but in Hungary, where my family's story, and mine, began.

But it wasn't just Leon and I who ate that chicken *paprikás,* or, later, studied the brooding paintings of Mihály Munkácsy at the Hungarian National Gallery or shopped on Váci utca or escaped from the city's hubbub on the tree-lined paths of Margaret Island in the middle of the Danube. Before me, only my cousin Suzie's father, my long-deceased Uncle Laci, had returned to Hungary. Judy had proposed more than once over the years that she and I travel to our homeland together, but I hadn't been ready then. My quest was still in the future, and I was concerned about being six thousand miles from home with her for a couple of weeks since our relationship still had its ups and downs. When I finally *was* ready, I knew it was Leon whom I needed by my side. Since Judy hadn't mentioned our going together for a number of years, I hoped she didn't mind that I didn't consider that possibility. So this trip was not just my trip. It was also a trip for Judy and my parents and Aunt Évi and Suzie and Nagymama and Nagypapa, all of whom, by choice or by chance, never returned. They shadowed me as Leon and I discovered Budapest. I watched and listened and spoke not only for myself, but for them.

* * *

Over the next week while we were in Budapest, Leon and I crossed and recrossed the Chain Bridge, under the pair of massive lion sculptures guarding either end, past the wide arcs of its suspension cables and the arched stone uprights supporting them, from Buda to Pest and back again. Walking on the sidewalks bordering its two lanes of cars, we sometimes stopped at mid-span to watch long, low tour boats gliding on the water or to savor the view of the verdant Buda hills to the west of the city. We admired the bridge outlined in lights from our hotel room after dark. If it's possible to fall in love with a bridge, I did; not only as a famed suspension bridge, one of Budapest's most popular landmarks, but also as a symbol of the link I hoped to establish with my heritage in Hungary.

On our second night, we had dinner at a sidewalk café on the riverbank in Pest and noticed that spotlights bathed the bridge in red and green. Approaching it on our way back to Buda, we soon found ourselves in a sea of people surging westward onto a deck cleared of cars.

"What's going on?" I asked a woman in Hungarian.

"It's a breast cancer walk," she told me, and I translated for Leon. As a longtime volunteer for the Fred Hutchinson Cancer Research Center in Seattle, I was pleased to learn that this popular means of increasing awareness of the disease and raising funds in the United States had found its way to Hungary.

"Let's do this in honor of Suzie," I suggested. My beloved cousin had been battling an aggressive form of breast cancer for four years, undergoing chemotherapy without a break that entire time. Our relationship had cooled in early adulthood, but we became close again when we were in our thirties, though she lived hundreds of miles from me in Havre.

"That's a great idea," he agreed. Swept along on the bridge by hundreds of people under purplish remnants of the sunset over Castle Hill, we marveled at the fierce determination that enabled my cousin to continue teaching fifth grade despite the onerous side effects of her treatments: baldness, nausea, joint pain, malaise. Her courage and zest for life inspired us.

Neither Leon nor I care for crowds. Yet walking on that bridge in my homeland, shoulder-to-shoulder with citizens who had also been touched in some way by this terrible disease, I felt a sense of peace and solidarity. My empathy for Suzie and her struggle swelled to encompass the struggles represented by all the people around me. My fellow Hungarians.

On the bridge and elsewhere, I reveled at my immersion in the Hungarian language. This Finno-Ugric language, related to only a handful of European languages, including Finnish and Estonian, is spoken by only fourteen million people in the world. For the first time in my life, I was in a place where what had most set me apart as a refugee child in Billings was the norm. I spoke Hungarian with everyone but Leon; read it on billboards and in brochures, magazines, and newspapers; listened to it on TV; eavesdropped on people speaking it on the street, in restaurants, on the subway. This language I had spoken for as long as I could remember made a city I was just getting to know seem deeply familiar.

I had underestimated the power of a shared language to create a bond, even with strangers. And it was only then that I realized just how much the language—even in light of my ambivalence—was an essential part of my identity.

There were also darker moments. Leon and I were crossing a street near the Margaret Bridge a few days after we arrived when a stooped man with greasy hair, wearing tattered pants and a soiled jacket, approached us from the opposite direction. Coming alongside me, he shook his fist toward Leon, on my other side. "Be verem a felyét," he growled in Hungarian. Leon, facing the other way, didn't notice.

"That guy who just passed us threatened to bash your head in," I whispered, tugging on his arm.

"Really? Let's get out of here," Leon answered, matching my quickened pace. I looked back at the man, mumbling to himself and obviously mentally ill, as we half-walked, half-ran to increase our distance from him.

"Is he gone?" Leon asked a short time later.

"No," I said. The man had turned and was following us, less than half a block away. Did his troubled mind perceive Leon as someone he knew, an enemy? I stole glances over my shoulder in the next block. The man was still there and moving closer. Whom could I ask for help? I saw no policemen. We crossed a busy street, and I turned again. The man was gone.

On one hand, I empathized with someone who clearly needed help, but my heart banged in my chest as I thought about what might have happened if he had carried a weapon and followed through with his threat.

I knew that a situation like this could happen anywhere, but my mother's words rang in my ears: "You have to be careful in Hungary." Before we left on our trip, she had told me about a family friend who, on a visit a few years earlier, met a Hungarian couple who drove him to a deserted field and robbed him of all his possessions, including the clothes he was wearing. "Don't forget what happened to Edit," she added. My father's cousin from Austria had left her locked car in the gated courtyard of a friend's house in Hungary while they had lunch. She went out afterward to find the car emptied of its contents and stripped of its parts.

At the time I wondered if my mother been trying to dissuade me from going to Hungary altogether. It was hard to know with her. I was often mystified by the nuances and innuendoes of her communication with me, at least partly a reflection of the Hungarian tendency to approach topics sideways rather than head-on. I knew her distrust of Hungary, even after the fall of Communism, ran deep. And she had seemed less interested in our travel plans than my father. Had she been worried only about our physical safety, as on our previous European trips? Or was she concerned about the effects on all of us of my digging into the past and reopening old wounds? In the end, her intent didn't matter. Headstrong like her, I was determined to go.

Since our arrival, I had been excited to the point of idealism about my homeland. The encounter with the man jolted me back to reality. Like the US or any other country, Hungary had its share of problems. Hard as it was to admit to myself, my mother's warnings had been valid, and I resolved to take them more seriously.

The encounter also gave me a sense of the fear my parents must have felt when the ÁVO, the Secret Police, stalked them before our escape. The officer who appeared at a nearby table when they went out to dinner. The car disguised as a Red Cross vehicle that parked in front of their house. The ÁVO's intimidation was subtler than that of a deranged man in rags muttering threats on the street; but instead of minutes, it lasted for weeks, keeping my parents off-balance as they agonized whether to try to escape, as they trembled at the prospect of a knock on the door in the middle of the night. Traces of those long-ago anxieties no doubt lingered in my mother's warning.

* * *

Budapest's kaleidoscope of sights and sounds and experiences eventually relegated the disturbing incident to the backs of our minds, and we resumed our avid sightseeing. A day or two later, on Castle Hill between the ornate Matthias Church, bastion of Hungarian Catholicism, and the Royal Palace, we saw a row of twenty flagpoles, each displaying a Hungarian flag. I felt a sudden surge of pride at the profusion of horizontal bands of red, white, and green, most familiar to me from the Hungarian Independence Day celebration of my childhood.

After touring the Hungarian National Gallery, we emerged from the Palace into a courtyard with beds of red and yellow begonias high above the Danube. Off to one side was a large gathering of men in business suits and women in cocktail dresses, talking and laughing, holding drinks, smoking cigarettes. Serving them were two young women with long blonde hair wearing traditional Hungarian costumes.

"Those outfits are just like the one Mom made for me!" I exclaimed to Leon. White dresses with full skirts, red velvet vests, and headdresses. Only the women's matching red boots set their costumes apart from mine; I'd had to settle for white flats and ankle socks.

"Do you want me to see if they'll let me take a picture of them?" Leon asked me.

I stared at the women, mesmerized, as though seeing an earlier incarnation of myself. "No," I answered, suddenly shy. I appreciated his offer, but hesitated to crash the party, to risk that his request might be rejected.

At the same time, I was amazed that, so far away in Billings, my mother had reproduced my costume down to the smallest twist of gold braid on red velvet. Perhaps she remembered a costume she had worn as a child. Or perhaps she drew on the collective memories of Nagymama and Aunt Évi and fellow refugee wives in Billings to figure out the details. After long hours cleaning other people's houses, how had she summoned the energy to sew the costume in the evenings on her antique Singer treadle sewing machine? Perhaps creating the costume transported her from being a refugee back to her carefree life in Hungary, a life she missed more than she cared to admit. No doubt she also hoped to teach me about my heritage and instill pride in me for my homeland. Then, all I cared about was wearing the beautiful articles of clothing. Now, I was finally ready to learn the lessons she had been trying to teach me, and to establish my own ties to Hungary.

One night toward the end of our stay, Leon and I lingered over dinner longer than we had planned at a restaurant several miles from where we were staying. I called a cab to take us back to our hotel, but after twenty minutes, there was no sign of it, and it was getting late. A waiter suggested that we take a bus instead and gave me directions to the stop. We stood on the street in an unfamiliar neighborhood at ten forty p.m., waiting for the last bus of the evening before service ended at eleven o'clock. Streetlights cast thin light partially blocked by trees. Traffic on the four-lane road next to us had dwindled to an occasional car whose headlights flashed on the surroundings before rushing past. Behind us yawned a park shrouded in complete darkness. A line of taxis waited for fares nearby, but our guidebook had been emphatic about the dangers of taking a cab waiting on the street instead of calling one. The drivers had a reputation for fleecing their customers. The lateness of the hour only magnified the risk, at least in my mind. This time, unlike at the airport, I decided to follow the guidebook's advice.

Scattered on the sidewalk around us were three or four young men in jeans, their faces indistinct in the dim light. Each seemed to be alone. I remembered the mentally ill man and my mother's warning. Would they suddenly converge into a group and try to rob us, a middle-aged American couple speaking English?

"I hope the bus comes soon," I whispered to Leon, shivering. The temperature had cooled from the unseasonable warmth of the day, and I had no jacket to wear over my knit top.

"It will," he said, ever the optimist. He wrapped an arm around me to try to warm me up, and I leaned against him. I tried not to think of what would happen if the bus didn't come—of our being stranded, walking for hours, searching for our hotel in a maze of dark streets, with danger, real or imagined, lurking.

We had no bus tickets since they could only be purchased

in advance at a bus station. Buses didn't accept cash, no doubt to discourage robbery. I didn't know the penalty for riding the bus without a ticket, for not paying a fare, but I imagined the driver accosting us and somehow discerning that we were foreigners. He would demand to see our passports. When he saw that I was born in Hungary, what would he do? My rational self told me he wouldn't do anything. Or maybe he'd kick us off the bus. I remembered the expressionless passport officer at the airport. Did the government keep track of people who had escaped from Hungary? Was there a file on my family in some office, ready to be activated at my first misstep? Again, I realized it was unlikely. But some of my parents' anti-Communist fervor had clearly rubbed off on me, and maybe vestiges of that authoritarian philosophy *did* remain in the current government. But it was also evident that my mother's warnings were feeding into a sense of danger far out of proportion to the actual situation we faced.

The bus arrived moments before eleven o'clock. Leon and I boarded with several others through the rear door. Seated in a semi-enclosure in front, the driver paid no attention to the passengers and didn't try to collect any tickets. We chose seats as far back as possible in the brightly lit coach to avoid attracting his attention for the rest of the trip. The bus started to move, and I pressed my forehead against the window, as though by doing so I could remove myself from a situation I found intensely uncomfortable. I tend to play by the rules, not defy them. We passed through dark, deserted streets. Shadowy buildings and trees were silhouetted against a cloudy, moonless sky. A dreamlike setting, stripped of any sense of time and place.

Into that void drifted the image of my mother, just twenty-four years old, cradling me in her arms during our escape. She, too, had boarded a bus under false pretenses, though in Soviet-occupied Austria. She and I had been in grave danger. If she hadn't trusted the roofer, Willi, to help us and had been caught, we would have been sent back to the ÁVO in Hungary. She might have ended up buried in an unmarked grave, or been broken by years in prison. And I might have been adopted by strangers and grown up under Communism. How brave my mother had been. How indebted I was to her. Could I have done what she did?

I wanted to think so, but the truth was, I had never faced a test remotely close to what she'd gone through. I didn't even have children. I'd avoided making not only a major sacrifice like hers, but all the other sacrifices, both large and small, routinely required of parents. Perhaps that life choice of mine was the source of the tension between my mother and me throughout my adulthood. Perhaps she resented that I could never truly understand and appreciate her sacrifices on my behalf because I hadn't made them myself as a mother with my own children. A formidable barrier between us.

After fifteen or twenty minutes, our bus turned onto the boulevard overlooking the Danube, with its reassuring sight of the Parliament building across the river in Pest. "Batthyány tér," the driver called a short time later, referring to a familiar square and transportation hub a few blocks from our hotel.

"Let's get off here," I whispered to Leon. I didn't know where the next stop was, and I didn't want to defraud the Budapest transit system any longer than necessary.

Strolling back to our hotel, we passed shuttered shops,

restaurants filled with loud voices and laughter, an occasional couple walking arm in arm. "See? Things worked out okay," Leon said as we arrived at the Victoria. "You worry too much."

"I know, but someone has to do it," I said, giving him a playful punch on the arm.

Budapest, in all its complexity, didn't always comply with my wish that our trip be flawless, but she was paving the way for my journey home.

chapter fourteen

Going Deeper

MAGDI, MY MOTHER'S cousin, was on a list of contacts in Budapest my parents gave us before we left on our trip. Also on it were my father's cousin, Lali, in her nineties, who lived in a nursing home, and a Hungarian family whose son had stayed with friends in Billings as an exchange student. I knew even before we left home that if I contacted anyone, it would be Magdi. This cousin with whom my mother and Aunt Évi seemed to have a close relationship, but who could also be a source of frustration, especially to my aunt, intrigued me.

One incident stood out. According to my mother, in the mid-1980s, Aunt Évi and Uncle Laci had treated Magdi and her husband, Béla, to a weekend in Las Vegas while they were in the United States visiting their older daughter, Kati, and her family. Kati had emigrated from Hungary after marrying her husband, a fellow Hungarian who was a US citizen. Her parents took advantage of a policy that allowed a certain number of citizens to travel outside the country each year with a limited amount of money, to ensure their return.

The weekend went well enough, but at one point, Magdi complained that they were eating all their meals at the hotel, instead of going to different restaurants. Aunt Évi interpreted her cousin's complaint as a lack of gratitude for their generosity, which had in fact strained their finances. She said nothing to Magdi at the time, but had shed hurt, angry tears on the plane flight home to Montana. Afterward, she complained to my mother, who tried to soothe her. Still, she continued to correspond with her cousin despite what had happened, only hinting at her ire with an occasional dig that Magdi sometimes returned.

"Magdi called Évi a white-haired grandmother," my mother reported to me on the phone one day. No matter that the comment was accurate; Aunt Évi had taken offense. My mother had had her own clashes with Aunt Évi, but she typically sided with her sister when it came to Magdi.

Was there more behind their ambivalence about their cousin than what had happened in Las Vegas? Perhaps my mother and aunt wondered why Magdi and Béla hadn't tried to escape from Hungary in 1956, along with two hundred thousand other citizens. Did my mother and aunt wonder about their politics? My mother never said. Regardless of where Magdi fell on the political spectrum, I was undeterred. I resolved to stay neutral, to not let anything I had heard from my mother or aunt color my impressions. I wanted to meet this daughter of my beloved Nagymama's younger sister, Paula, the closest remaining tie to my mother's side of the family in Hungary.

I stood at the window of our room at the Hotel Victoria midway through our week in the city, admiring the view as the lights of Budapest and the Chain Bridge came on in the deepening dusk. Leon and I had returned from a late dinner at the Angelika, an open-air café near the hotel, but it was too early to go to sleep. Turning from the window, I picked up the TV remote control and started flipping through channels. Most programs were in German, whose basics were all I remembered from high school and college classes.

"I think I'll call Magdi," I said to Leon, who was lying on the bed engrossed in a mystery. I had located her address on a city map and discovered she lived in the district of Óbuda, just a few miles north of our hotel.

"Go for it," he said, turning a page.

"I'm nervous … I wonder how she'll react."

He looked up from his book. "She'll probably be thrilled to hear from you," he said.

I picked up the receiver and dialed the unfamiliar configuration of numbers. My stomach clenched as I listened to ringing that sounded like a busy signal at home. I remembered that my parents had asked me not to tell Magdi or other friends and relatives in Hungary about their diminished fortunes in the United States, about Robie's disability. I wondered what my mother had told Magdi about our family in her many years of letters. Perhaps Magdi, as Omama had, knew more about our family than she revealed. "You have nothing to be ashamed of," I had argued to my parents. They had worked hard, provided for their family, done their best under overwhelming circumstances. I also resisted perpetuating my family's code of silence at a time when I was striving to communicate more openly about sensitive subjects in my own life.

"We'd be ridiculed," my father said. His statement puzzled me. Why would a relative, someone who supposedly cared about us, fail to empathize that my parents' lives in America hadn't worked out quite as they had hoped? Was this a personal issue, or an ideological one? Were my parents trying to provide a positive image of capitalism to someone who had lived under Communism? I didn't know. But my parents were adamant, and I reluctantly agreed to say nothing. If Magdi asked questions I couldn't answer truthfully, I would refer her back to my parents. Still, I've never been good at dissembling. Would I be able to deflect difficult questions, especially in Hungarian? A lively female voice interrupted my musings. "Hallo?"

"Magdi néni?" I asked, hesitant.

"Igen." (Yes.)

"This is Erika, Vilmy's daughter, from America," I said in Hungarian. I stumbled over the words, but was glad that I remembered to address her as *néni* (aunt), a term of respect used with a woman older than the speaker, regardless of the actual relationship.

"Erika!" she exclaimed in an accent that was pure Budapest. She sounded as delighted as anyone ever had to hear from me. "Your mother wrote last year that you were coming, but I didn't believe it."

"It took a while, but my husband, Leon, and I are finally here," I said. "Can we see you?"

"Of course!"

As we chatted, Magdi marveled at my command of Hungarian. I liked her already. My confidence in my Hungarian language skills also went up a notch. We arranged to meet at our hotel the next day and go to lunch.

* * *

When Leon and I entered the lobby at twelve thirty, Magdi was waiting. A widow in her late seventies, she was perhaps five feet tall, with a body stout through the middle, but with slender limbs. She wore a loose top covered with bold red, yellow, and turquoise flowers and a white skirt and sandals. Strawberry blonde bobbed hair framed her round face. I would have known her anywhere, and not just from the photographs in my mother's albums. Looking into Magdi's blue eyes, set in shadowed skin behind glasses with beige plastic frames, was like looking into Nagymama's eyes.

We greeted each other and hugged as though we had known each other forever. I introduced Leon and we sank onto one of the two leather couches near the reception desk that filled the tiny lobby. We chattered and exchanged photos, mine of my parents, Judy and her family, and Aunt Évi and Suzie and her family; hers of Kati and her husband and two children. She said she hoped we would meet her younger daughter, little Magdi, and her husband, Tibor, who also lived in Budapest, during our stay. I was relieved that her questions about our family focused on the present, on how people were doing. "Fine," I said. It was mostly true. I didn't mention Suzie's breast cancer. Aunt Évi, who corresponded with relatives in Hungary on behalf of herself and my cousin, had asked me not to reveal her illness. I knew better than to argue.

Magdi's rapid speech and animated gestures made her seem younger than her age, and our excited voices echoed in the cramped space. After recommending Le Jardin de Paris on the next street over for lunch, Gaby shooed us out to make room for other guests.

I would have preferred a Hungarian restaurant but didn't want to ask Magdi to walk too far. She had ridden the bus from her home to meet us, and I knew she'd had health problems, including a major surgery a number of years earlier. She never mentioned it. Did all Hungarians avoid painful topics, or was it just our family? We sat at a round metal table with matching chairs in the shade of trees turning color, surrounded by clusters of bamboo like those in our yard at home. The menu included a few Hungarian entrees, and we lingered over a combination of French and Hungarian dishes and desserts—goulash and French onion soup and crème brûlée and sour cherry tart—until midafternoon.

Magdi, reminiscing about childhood visits with my mother and Aunt Évi in Vasvár during summer vacations, had only good things to say about her cousins. "I looked up to them," she said. Small wonder, since Aunt Évi was five years older than she was, and my mother, seven. I wanted to know her impressions of them, how they had behaved toward her, but Magdi only shared with me that they were always well-dressed. Pressing her for details felt as though it would be disloyal to my mother and aunt, and I was worried that my doing so might trigger questions about the past that I hoped Magdi wouldn't ask me. I let her take the lead in our conversation.

"Are you going to Szombathely and Vasvár from here?" she asked.

"Yes," I told her. "I can't wait to see where I was born and where Mom grew up."

"I recently went to both places," she said. "You must go to Szentkut (Holy Well) when you're in Vasvár." My mother had already asked me to try to find the religious shrine in a forest where Nagymama and Nagypapa took her and Aunt Évi on outings as children.

"Why is it called that?" I asked.

"Long ago, a blind man went there and bathed his eyes in water from the well. Afterward, he could see."

"What a wonderful story," I said. Magdi was a devout Catholic, but as a lapsed Congregationalist who has dabbled in Buddhism, I appreciated the tale more as legend than as of any religious significance.

"Szombathely recently renovated its main square and it's even more beautiful than before," Magdi said. I felt even more eager to see my birthplace. As we talked, I periodically translated for Leon. He didn't seem to mind his limited role in the conversation; he's not a talkative person and was accustomed to my lapsing into Hungarian during visits with my parents. Listening to Magdi's Budapest accent, I found myself starting to emulate it. Another step in my language assimilation.

Our conversation shifted to the economy, the focus of protests in Budapest Leon and I read about in *The Seattle Times* shortly before we left home. Hungarians had learned that the prime minister, Ferenc Gyurcsány, had lied about the country's economic woes several months earlier in order to win reelection. At the same time, they were feeling the impact of tax increases and austerity measures later instituted to address the problem. Ten thousand mostly peaceful protesters took to the streets near Parliament and the State television station, but a small group turned violent, burning cars and vandalizing buildings. Police in riot gear deployed water cannons. By the time we arrived, the protests had ended, but Magdi confirmed that the conditions that caused them had not.

"Times are hard here," she said, leaning forward and speaking in a lowered voice.

"I can imagine."

"The tax increases are killing me. I'm retired, but my taxes go up because they tax everything, even goods and services. My utilities went up 18 percent this year."

"I'm sorry to hear that," I said.

"Financially at least, life was easier for me under Communism," she said. She studied me, her eyes narrowed, as though gauging my reaction.

"I can see why it might have been," I said, choosing my words carefully. How could I disagree, despite the anti-Communist attitudes I had inherited from my parents?

Magdi complained of American corporations that took advantage of Hungary's five-year moratorium on taxes to encourage investment by foreign companies, only to pull out of the country when the period lapsed. I was dismayed to hear that fellow Americans were exploiting my homeland, my first sense of divided loyalties.

"Our prime minister calls himself a socialist, but he's really a Communist in disguise," Magdi continued, her voice edged with contempt. "Socialists are just holdover Communists. And the people who elect them are the older generation who suffered under Communism!" In that moment, any questions I might have had about her politics evaporated. I was pleased to hear that she shared my parents' and my aversion toward Communism, that we had something so significant in common.

"I promised myself I wouldn't talk about politics because I get so angry," Magdi said, sheepish.

"I get upset, too," I said. "But that never keeps me from a political discussion." When Magdi described President George W. Bush's trip to Budapest, complete with emptied streets and sharpshooters stationed on buildings, I made no effort to conceal my disdain for him and his administration. "Talking politics must be in our genes, because Nagymama liked it, too," I said. Magdi and I smiled at each other. A bond was growing between us.

* * *

She invited us to visit her in Óbuda the following afternoon. Leon and I arrived early at the charming main square lined with sherbet-colored Baroque buildings where she would meet us. We whiled away an hour in the hot sun sitting outside at a bistro, snacking on sausage and cheese and *palacsinta*, flat crepes filled with ground walnuts that we decided weren't quite as tasty as those my mother made. We watched several wedding parties—brides in billows of white, grooms in dark suits, pastel-clad guests, cars decorated with flowers instead of tin cans and sayings—arriving to register the marriages at the city hall next door. Magdi fetched us as the sun slanted over tile roofs, casting shadows on the cobblestones.

"Hello, hello," she said, lively as the day before, though she'd mentioned that her blood pressure was acting up. "Little Magdi and Tibor will drive us to Szentendre later," she said, referring to a tourist town north of Budapest on the Danube. "You must see it. And we'll eat dinner at the Uj Sipós Halászkert afterward." The fish restaurant was across the square from where Leon and I had been sitting. I had hoped for a change of scene, but Magdi had clearly made up her mind. We stopped at the restaurant and made a reservation for later that evening.

Magdi's apartment building, one of several massive gray concrete Communist-era structures in the vicinity, was across a four-lane freeway from the square. We walked there via a tunnel underneath, passing Roman ruins, knee-high remnants of stone walls with concrete ramps curving over them in a fascinating juxtaposition of the ancient and modern. At her building, Magdi unlocked the front door, and we entered a stark space that smelled vaguely of cooking, perhaps cabbage or goulash. A groaning elevator deposited us on the fifth floor, where a door with bars that could have come from a jail cell separated the elevator lobby from her hallway. She unlocked it without comment. Leon and I exchanged uneasy glances as we crossed to the hall, and it clanged shut behind us.

Magdi's tidy, two-bedroom, lace-curtained apartment was cozy and inviting. Amid antiques and doilies and family photographs in her living room, she plied us with tasty cheese sticks and *püspök kenyér*, a Hungarian fruitcake that she had baked for us.

"Eat," she urged us. We didn't have the heart to tell her we had just eaten, so we ate. We also chatted about Leon's and my outing to Margaret Island earlier in the day, where we had enjoyed a respite from the city's hubbub in open spaces lined with multicolored flowers and on shaded paths among couples and families enjoying the sunny warm Saturday. When we realized we had walked the length of the island and were across the Árpád Bridge from Óbuda, we decided to go there directly, rather than returning to our hotel and taking a bus.

"Let's surprise your parents with a phone call," Magdi suggested. I quickly calculated that with the eight-hour time difference, it was nine a.m. in Billings. My father would be up, but my mother tended to sleep late because of her rheumatoid arthritis and would barely be awake. Still, Magdi's generous offer touched me, and I reluctantly agreed. I dialed the number and when my mother answered, I handed the phone to Magdi.

"Vilmy, it's Magdi. I'm thrilled that Erika and Leon are here with me in Budapest," she said. With great enthusiasm, she relayed the details of our visit the day before. Then she handed the phone to me.

"It's been fun getting to know Magdi," I said in Hungarian, so our hostess would know what I was saying.

"Good!" my father said, listening on the extension at their end. My mother was noncommittal, a reaction I attributed to the early hour. Concerned about the cost of the call to Magdi, I soon said goodbye. More detailed phone calls with my parents would come later, when we could speak privately instead of in earshot of a relative I had just met the day before. And it would be easier to talk with them not in the pure Hungarian I needed to use in front of Magdi, but in the mixture of Hungarian and English that we used when we spoke with each other.

Little Magdi and Tibor arrived a short time later. She was a few years younger than me, with short, sandy hair and her father's Roman nose. Greeting us, she was as lively and engaging as her mother, traits no doubt useful in her high-level job at a shipping firm. Her chiffon flowered skirt, sleeveless top, and strappy sandals made me feel dowdy in my black pants and knit top, wilted from our long walk earlier in the day. "You look just like your mother," she told me, though she would have seen her only in photographs. She even called me "Vilmy" a couple of times during the evening. Tibor, mustached and balding, was friendly, but less outgoing than his wife. Leon had been eagerly awaiting their arrival since little Magdi speaks some English. But she soon revealed that she was suffering from a bad toothache, and most of her comments after that were about how much it hurt.

She drove us to Szentendre, a half hour away, a town as picturesque as Magdi had promised, with ornate Baroque buildings and cobblestones winding up a hill. But at six thirty on a Saturday evening, only a few tourists remained and most of the stores were closing. We climbed up to the Serbian Orthodox church on the crest and entered through a side door. The spare notes of a Gregorian chant emanated from behind a screen, and I was reminded of my Russian Nagypapa. He had practiced the Greek Orthodox faith, part of the same overarching Eastern Orthodox religion, with similar beliefs. My grandfather, who was Magdi's uncle by marriage, had been gruff and impatient with me during my childhood, and I avoided him. But I did enjoy watching him from a distance in the backyard of his and Nagymama's house next door to us in Billings, a gray fedora jammed on his head as he noodled on his harmonica or pruned rosebushes while smoking a cigar.

Only years after his death, digging in the dirt of my own backyard, did I begin to feel a bond with a grandfather who had made his living in Billings as a gardener under the supervision of the black-robed Sisters of Charity at St. Vincent Hospital. He never learned to speak English beyond a few words—in fact, he wasn't even fluent in Hungarian—but somehow he and the nuns managed to communicate enough that he kept the grounds looking immaculate. I admired that he had built a new life in Billings with my grandmother when he was over sixty years old, and that he nursed her for several years during her decline after a stroke. Though he was six years older than she was, they died just sixteen days apart. Nagymama passed away in a nursing home of a heart attack; he was suffering from cancer, and my mother and aunt decided not to add to his burden by telling him. But somehow, deep inside, he must have sensed her passing, and he couldn't face going on without her.

I imagined that chanting monks in hooded robes were prompting my thoughts of my grandfather in the hilltop church, though the haunting music was no doubt a recording. Still, it inspired me to view my grandfather not just as someone who made me uneasy as a child, but as the multidimensional person that he was, someone also to be admired and to be missed. The half-moon hanging in the sky turning indigo over the town's red tile roofs seemed to affirm my epiphany.

Back in Óbuda at the fish restaurant, the host seated us in a room connected to the main dining area by French doors. We sat at a long table covered in a white tablecloth, ivory candles in silver candlesticks, wine glasses, china plates decorated with calla lilies, and tastefully simple silverware. The private room, grander than the rest of the establishment, appeared to be the only place where the restaurant could accommodate our request for a nonsmoking area because of Leon's asthma. Smoking is allowed in many public places in Hungary, and this restaurant, hazy with smoke, was no exception. I sat between the two Magdis on one side of the table and Leon and Tibor sat opposite us. Our waiter soon arrived, a brawny man in black pants and a white shirt who, though friendly enough, could easily have been mistaken for a street thug. Dark hair slicked straight back topped a wide face with coarse features. We all ordered white wine, except little Magdi, who asked for water so she could take a pain pill for her steadily worsening toothache.

The waiter returned a few minutes later. But instead of our drinks, he carried a platter with three large, dark gray fish, their lifeless tails flopping over the edge. "Our specialty is fish," he announced in Hungarian. "You must order it." The two Magdis immediately opted out, settling on *turós tészta,* noodles with cottage cheese, a popular Hungarian dish. That left Tibor, Leon, and me to meet the waiter's demand.

"What do you think of the waiter's fish?" Tibor asked me.

"I have no idea," I said, adding that Leon and I were more familiar with ocean fish like salmon. "You decide."

Tibor hesitated. "You might not like what I order."

"Don't worry about it," I said. The waiter remained rooted to the spot, clutching the platter. It was clear he wasn't going anywhere until we ordered fish.

I looked at Leon. "What shall we do?" I asked him. "We don't know anything about these fish, and Tibor doesn't want to decide. At this rate, we'll be here all night."

"Tell him to pick something that doesn't taste too fishy," Leon suggested.

I passed the message to Tibor, who finally settled on the *Balatoni süllő*, a variety of perch from Lake Balaton. When the waiter finally left to put in our orders, I joked that the chef must have banned him from the kitchen until he got rid of at least some of the fish on the platter. Tibor and the two Magdis, and Leon, after I translated, all laughed. I was proud of myself for pulling off a joke in Hungarian.

A Gypsy band—a man playing a *cimbalom,* a Hungarian dulcimer; a bass player; and a roving violinist—was entertaining a crowd growing increasingly raucous in the main room. Maudlin singing. Bursts of laughter. Eating the mild, delicious *süllő* baked in parchment, I remembered another Gypsy band, the band that had entertained my parents in Szombathely on June 20, 1948, the eve of my father and Judy's escape. I told Magdi how my father sang "I'm Leaving Your Village" along with the band in the presence of the ÁVO officer trailing him and my mother.

Magdi, who hadn't heard the story, laughed and clapped her hands, delighted. "I know that song," she said. She beckoned the balding, dark-eyed violinist in a blue vest over to our table and asked him to play it. He leaned toward us, drawing his bow over the strings to produce the first melancholy notes. His rich baritone mingled with Magdi's quavering soprano, another echo of Nagymama, as they sang the words of love and loss and regret. Picking up the tune, I started to hum along, but the lump forming in my throat soon stopped me. I started to cry. My companions smiled at me in empathy, and Leon handed me his white handkerchief. Magdi put her arm around me and pulled me close. In that moment, the present merged with my parents' past. Listening to the song my father had so bravely flung in the face of authority before we escaped, I could feel, as never before, the fear, the doubt, the sadness he and my mother must have felt as they faced leaving behind their homeland and people they loved, forever.

chapter fifteen

In My Birthplace

LEON AND I had been riding the train westward from Budapest for almost three hours. Rolling past our window were fields of sunflowers and spent cornstalks alternating with fallow land, and an occasional low hill covered with deciduous trees that had yet to turn color in early October. The train slowed as the industrial areas on the outskirts came into view, and at four twenty, it rolled to a stop in the station. When I spotted the rectangular blue sign with yellow letters spelling "Szombathely," my eyes blurred with tears. My years of research, of questioning my parents and recording their responses, of poring over maps, of studying photographs and documents and drawings, had culminated in this moment. I was finally back in the place where I came into the world. What would I discover in this city with its vestiges of our former lives?

We emerged from a Renaissance-style station that, from the street, looked just like the photograph in my mother's book of old Szombathely postcards, freshly painted tan with off-white trim. It was in the shadow of this building that my parents, shortly before their own journeys of escape, had encountered the group of failed escapees captured at the border. One wrong word, one wrong move, and we, too, might have ended up in this spot guarded by soldiers with rifles. The ghosts of those long-ago victims floated around passengers rolling their suitcases on the sidewalk, around cars and taxis pulling up to the building, around us. I shivered, though the afternoon was warm.

Our lodgings were at the twelve-room Hotel Wagner, a charming pink stucco inn with ivy spilling from its window boxes. Several congenial young men in white shirts and black trousers staffed the front desk of the hotel and the tavern/restaurant on the premises. None of them spoke English. Suddenly, my speaking Hungarian was no longer optional. I was relieved to switch from the quasi-Budapest accent I had begun to acquire from Magdi to the familiar Vas Megye accent they all spoke. "How do you pronounce the name of this town?" I asked them.

"Sōmbŏt-high," one of them answered, confirming how my family had always pronounced it. Most Budapest-accented Hungarians I met in the United States had corrected me when I'd told them where I was from, saying it was pronounced "Sōmbŏt-hāy." I felt vindicated. Who would know better how to pronounce the name of the town than the people who lived there?

The desk clerk assigned us to a spacious second-floor room at the head of the stairs with high ceilings, a built-in-desk, and a painting of sunflowers over the queen-sized bed. After we unpacked, I pulled aside the sheer curtain at one of the casement windows and looked down on the street. Like the square behind Parliament in Budapest and many streets and landmarks in Hungary, it was named for the national hero of the 1800s, Kossuth Lajos. Lining it on both sides were two- and three-story buildings painted pastel colors. Diagonally across from us was No. 4, in whose upstairs apartment Aunt Évi, Uncle Laci, and my cousin Suzie had lived before they escaped during the 1956 Revolution. Leon and I had chosen the Wagner because of its proximity to the former Reich house and factory. That it was even closer to where Suzie and her parents had lived was an unexpected bonus.

When we later strolled down the street, we learned that the first floor of the building was occupied by a real estate firm, Engel & Volkers. Displayed in large windows were photographs of houses and commercial buildings for sale for millions of forints since Hungary, though part of the European Union, was not yet on the euro. The prices sounded high, but since the exchange rate at the time was more than two hundred forints to one US dollar, they were mostly $100,000 or less, quite reasonable by our standards. But to Hungarians coping with a shaky economy, they were likely just as expensive as they first seemed.

I imagined my cousin as a young child, skipping on the sidewalk with her friends or jumping rope while Aunt Évi, and Uncle Laci when he wasn't away at his job with the railroad, chatted with neighbors or leaned out an upstairs window to watch her. Was it here where Suzie was threatened by a Soviet soldier during the Revolution? My parents had mentioned the incident, but I had never asked Suzie for details. She and I rarely talked about the past, and although I was curious about what had happened, I didn't want to add to her trauma by asking her to relive it. But standing in the vicinity of where the encounter might have occurred, I imagined an event in November 1956 that no doubt contributed to the shy, frightened demeanor of the girl I met just a few months later.

Clouds of dust hang over a street too narrow for tanks, over piles of rubble and façades of buildings pitted with bullet holes. In the distance, the sound of an occasional gunshot, of people yelling. Soviet soldiers mill among residents who walk quickly, their heads lowered to avoid attracting attention to themselves. Suzie, eight years old, has seen the chaos in the streets. She has seen how her parents, like her teacher and other adults, have grown tense and wary, their eyes filled with fear. She has heard them talking in hushed voices with an undertone of hope about the uprising, about trying to drive the Soviets out of Hungary. But she doesn't really understand.

On the way home from school one day, she glances at a young Soviet soldier, perhaps wondering how he fits into a world turned upside down. He looks back at her. Compassion flickers in his eyes before they turn cold. He lifts his rifle, aiming it at Suzie's slender body wrapped in a wool coat. A frozen tableau of two figures, soldier and child, staring at each other. She, terrified. He, arrogant? Amused? Bored? He mutters something in Russian, then lowers his rifle and waves her away. Suzie runs from him, up the stairs to her apartment, crying for her parents. Did my cousin realize how lucky she was that the soldier didn't shoot? I shuddered at the thought of it. How empty my childhood would have been without her.

Next to the real estate office, an open gate led to a courtyard and a green, weedy lawn with a couple of scrubby evergreens where Suzie might have played with her friends. Stairs covered in gray slate led to the second floor. I wanted to climb them, to echo the hundreds of trips Suzie and her parents made up and down them in the years they lived there. But I wasn't sure whether we were even supposed to be inside the gate. If I climbed the stairs, would I be accused of trespassing? In the end, I confined myself to taking photographs from every angle, so Suzie and Aunt Évi could see how much the outside of their former home had changed—or not.

Leon and I discovered that Szombathely, ten miles from the Austrian border, was still the agricultural and industrial center it had been in 1948, but its population had more than doubled, to ninety thousand. Hungary's oldest city, it was established in AD 43 by the emperor Claudius as a Roman outpost, Savaria. Extensive ruins from that settlement were now open to the public, but few tourists visited them. Most of the visitors were bargain-hunting Austrians. Rather than souvenir stores and tourist information sites, we found "Kina" stores offering discount goods from China, no doubt a boon both to Austrians and to residents struggling in the poor economy.

At the east end of the block occupied by our hotel and Suzie's former home was the city's Fő Tér, the recently remodeled main square that Magdi had mentioned, a feature of larger Hungarian towns, anchored by a Catholic church. The Franciscan Church (later renamed St. Elizabeth Church) marked the far end of the triangular space, two blocks long, where Szombathely's citizens came to see and be seen, to learn what was happening, to attend festivals and celebrations. One night early in our weeklong stay, perhaps a hundred people clustered around a speaker under a hazy moon to learn that the right-leaning opposition, the Fidesz Party, had made significant gains in recent elections. Several listeners clutched small Hungarian flags waving gently in the breeze, a sight that moved me. Those flags were a powerful symbol of the contrast between the conditions before our escape—the country in the stranglehold of a Soviet-backed regime growing ever more repressive—and the present, with the country's leaders chosen by a free people.

Benches were scattered around the square for sitting and people-watching, and several fountains among small trees shot intermittent arcs of water into the air. Lining the edges of the pavement were restaurants and shops selling flowers and shoes and clothing, one with a sign advertising "farmers," the Hungarian term for jeans. We were surprised to see a bronze statue of James Joyce emerging from a white stucco wall on the south side of the square. A souvenir book later revealed that Joyce had modeled Leopold Bloom, the main character of *Ulysses,* on a man named Blum from Szombathely, whom he met while living in Trieste. I was delighted that my birthplace was linked to such a prominent author and literary work, and that it had chosen to honor him in this way. But then, Hungary places a high value on writers and literature. Time and again, I learned that if a street or square wasn't named after a national hero, it was named after a poet or writer.

* * *

On the north side of the square at Kőszeg street was a jewelry store that was once the site of the Palace Café. Before World War II, my Omama met the wives of other engineers there for coffee and smoked an occasional cigarette, near-scandalous behavior in those days. *Way to go, Omama,*

I thought as we strolled by the building. This grandmother I had known only through her letters had always struck me as staid and conventional, but my discussions with my father had revealed that she had a rebellious streak, like me.

She and Opapa and my parents had worshipped at the Evangélikus templom, the Lutheran church whose spire was visible from the west end of the street where we were staying. On a Sunday morning a day or two after we arrived in town, Leon and I crossed Freedom Fighters Street with its heavy traffic and a bridge over the sluggish, canal-like Perint River to approach the off-white building dominated by a tall steeple in a cluster of trees at the far end of the block. Men in suits and women in dresses walked up the stairs for a ten a.m. worship service. We followed them into a sanctuary more austere than those of the Catholic churches we had seen. A large oil painting of an angel in white hung in a gold frame behind a communion table covered with a white cloth and a candle on either side of a gold cross. The church was also smaller, with only ten or twelve rows separated by a red-carpeted center aisle.

My parents had described their wedding here as a simple affair, with only their parents and a few relatives and friends in attendance. I imagined them standing at the altar with a minister in a black robe presiding. My mother wore a skirted suit, rather than a white wedding gown and veil, as she and my father promised to love, honor, and cherish each other, with no inkling of the trials that lay ahead. Less than a year later, in the wake of the factory takeover, they stood in the same spot, my mother holding me in a white, lace-trimmed christening dress as the minister blessed me and traced a cross on my forehead with holy water. In the weeks after my baptism, they sat in the pews with Omama and Opapa on Sunday mornings, singing hymns and listening to sermons and praying for God's mercy as their lives disintegrated.

Leon and I decided against staying for a worship service. He would understand nothing, and ecclesiastical Hungarian would present a challenge even for me. As we turned to leave, the organist began to play what I remembered from my ten years in the choir at First Congregational Church in Billings as the Doxology after the offering: "Praise God from whom all blessings flow; praise him all creatures here below ...." I hummed the tune with tears in my eyes as the sound of voices singing the hymn with Hungarian lyrics followed us out the door and down the stairs. Emotions buried for a lifetime were rising to the surface, spilling out again and again, beyond my control. I felt an ever-growing connection to my homeland and my family's history.

Omama and Opapa's home, where I was born and where we lived before our escape, was down the block from the church on Dózsa Győrgy utca, a quiet, tree-lined street named for a fifteenth-century revolutionary. I recognized the house right away from the 1980s photograph taken by a family friend. The length of the large, one-story structure faced the street. Like most of the buildings in the center of Szombathely, it abutted its neighbors, a school on one side and a sheet metal business on the other. A roof of mottled red and black tile topped a façade of varying shades of disintegrating ocher stucco, marred with graffiti. No evidence remained of the grandeur my parents had described. Still, I longed to see more. Three square, lace-curtained windows were set too high in the wall to permit even a peek inside. What had once been an arched wooden gateway leading to a courtyard had been transformed into a glass-paneled door flanked by two windows. Leon and I peered in, but shelves and curtains obscured what lay in the darkness beyond.

"Do you think this is still used as an entrance?" I asked him.

"I doubt it," he said, trying to turn a handle that didn't budge.

Since the house seemed deserted, it didn't occur to us to try to knock to get inside. Instead, I paced back and forth on the sidewalk, as though by breathing the air around the house I could somehow discern its contents. The light blue building to the north would have been part of the factory's original site, perhaps the offices where my mother worked as the payroll clerk. But from what my parents had told me, we needed to view the buildings from inside the house or the courtyard to get a true sense of what the factory had been like in their day. That seemed impossible.

Discouraged, we walked two blocks west to the buildings of the former factory's second location, Plant B, the iron foundry where my father had supervised a hundred employees. The original factory gate with the "Reich Gépgyár" sign was long gone. In its place was a chain-link gate, with the word, "Öntöde," or foundry, spelled out in letters of red, yellow, blue, and green in an arch above it. The area, still referred to by that name, was now a complex of offices, apartments, a gym, a café. White buildings of one and two stories, the frame of each window painted a different primary color, lined the street, and behind them rose the factory's original smokestack, ringed in faded shades of the letters above the gate. One of these buildings—perhaps the one-story structure faced with river stones—had been the scene of the meeting where the Communist Ligeti, in minutes, had stripped my grandfather of all he had built over three decades of his life. Opapa would have walked on these streets with their tidy houses afterward, his mind no doubt reeling from his public humiliation and banishment.

Farther on, Leon and I came to St. Stephen's Park, namesake of Hungary's first king and its patron saint—a narrow, wooded area alongside a busy thoroughfare. Omama and Opapa had strolled here on their daily walks, and this is where I imagined he came to collect his thoughts after the factory takeover, to decide what to do next. All that remained of the tall water fountain adorned with cherubs was a wide basin in the ground filled with white rocks and circled with red, pink, and yellow flowers and low shrubs. Mirroring the way my parents' and grandparents' lives must have felt at the end of that fateful day, the park was empty.

chapter sixteen

Betrayal

Like Magdi in Budapest, Marinka, the widow of Sónyi, my father's best friend from childhood, was the person I most wanted to see in Szombathely. But talking with her on the phone for the first time wasn't as easy it had been with Magdi. Marinka was eighty-seven years old, and her voice was soft and low, with a plaintive tone that suggested she might be depressed. Because she was of my parents' generation and a stranger to me, etiquette dictated that I speak to her in the formal manner of Hungarian. That meant I needed to address her in the third person, rather than the second. Doing so can be tricky, because at least in the traditional form of the language my parents taught me, you are also to avoid any actual reference to the person as a subject. That's possible only because, in Hungarian, the subject of a sentence isn't necessarily a separate word, as it is in English. "How are you?" becomes "Hogy van?" if you're being formal and "Hogy vagy?" if you're not, with the second word incorporating both the subject and the verb. My experience with "*magázni*," as the practice is called, was limited, since I spoke Hungarian mostly with my parents. Using it to try to establish rapport with Marinka, I floundered and hesitated, fumbling for words. Finally she took pity on me. "Hivjál engemet Marinka néni" (Call me Aunt Marinka), she said, signaling that I could speak to her informally. The tension eased.

I hoped that Marinka could provide insights into the events prior to our 1948 escape, and that she also might have documents about the factory of interest to my father. He had helped Sónyi secure a white-collar job at the factory, though he had been a poor student. Sónyi had spent his entire career there, first under Opapa, and after the factory takeover, the Communists. When my parents told Marinka that we would be in Szombathely, she had offered to show us around, and I was eager to learn more from someone who lived there.

Leon and I met her a couple of days after our phone call in her street-level apartment in a drab, four-story concrete building across the street from Szombathely's main library. From there, we would visit the cemetery where Opapa was buried and the former Reich house and factory before going out to lunch. Marinka greeted us warmly at her front door on an open hallway overlooking a parking lot. Her movements were slow and deliberate, but her short, curly gray hair framed a round face with brown eyes that seemed full of life. "Come sit," she said, gesturing toward a small round table in her living room bathed in sunlight from a south-facing window. She offered us cookies and rum balls rolled in coconut that she had made in our honor, and we sampled them with gusto.

The living room was not unlike Magdi's, with its antiques and lace curtains and figurines and doilies, except for a bold splash of color from a sofa upholstered in red fabric. Adjoining the room through a wide doorway was a bedroom filled with two twin beds placed end-to-end. A small kitchen and bathroom completed the space. I was astonished that Marinka had also proposed to my parents that, rather than booking a room in a hotel, Leon and I stay with her. We prefer our privacy and had politely refused. Seeing how cramped her apartment was confirmed the wisdom of our decision.

Marinka studied Leon as I introduced them. "He looks like a good man," she said. When I translated for Leon, my modest spouse blushed. I silently commended Marinka for being so perceptive.

Our conversation began with the cemetery that would be our first stop. "Sónyi is also buried there," Marinka said, adding that she worried about his grave. She'd had it sandblasted several times but had recently been told it couldn't be done again, for fear of wearing the stone away. "I wonder who will tend the grave after I die," she said. At her advanced age, with no children, she had lost all her relatives and no doubt most of her friends. I felt sad for her—for her loneliness, for the narrowing of her outlook to the grave she would likely soon also occupy. I knew from my parents that, unlike Leon and me, Marinka and Sónyi had not been childless by choice. But I still had the fleeting sensation that I was catching a glimpse of my own future.

"What were my Omama and Opapa like?" I asked her, eager to change the subject. Marinka's face, which had been somber to that point, broke into a broad smile.

"They were both kind, wonderful people," she said, though she was more familiar with Opapa since he was her husband's employer. She described him as well over six feet tall and unusually slender. He rode everywhere on a bicycle, a detail my parents had never mentioned. "I'm so grateful your grandfather hired Sónyi at the factory," she said.

"Who knows where he might have ended up otherwise?" Hearing someone outside my family echo my parents' praise of Omama and Opapa increased my conviction that despite how things ended, my grandparents had been respected in this community. I smiled back at her.

Every year, at my parents' request, Marinka took flowers to Opapa's grave on All Saints' Day, November 1, just a few weeks hence. I was to give her the money this year so my parents wouldn't need to send it. "I'd like to put flowers on the grave today, too," I told her.

"Don't," Marinka said. "The wind will just blow them away." She explained to us that she tucked her flowers into a wreath that anchored them to the grave. "Take a candle instead."

I felt a flash of resentment. Why was she discouraging me from honoring my grandfather the way I wanted? Still, I wasn't going to argue with someone I had just met. I suddenly remembered my father's request. "Do you have any documents from the Reich Gépgyár?" I asked her.

"No … the war …" Marinka replied, shaking her head. It seemed plausible that documents she might have had from the years before the takeover had been lost or destroyed, perhaps during the bombing of Szombathely by the Allies in 1945. But Marinka looked uncomfortable, and there was an awkward pause. Was she hiding something? I couldn't tell, but I decided not to force the issue.

* * *

We drove to the cemetery covering several acres on the southwest side of town in our compact rental car, a Spanish Seat whose model name, to Leon's and my delight, was also Leon. A funeral was in progress, requiring us to park outside the gates. We stopped at the flower shop near the entrance, and I looked with longing at pails filled with multicolored blooms before choosing a candle in a jar for Opapa's grave. Marinka guided us southward past the scene of the service, a round domed chapel covered in charcoal ray tiles. We walked on a pathway lined with evergreens and formally pruned hedges, past stone crypts extending several inches to a foot or more above ground, the preferred method of burial in Hungary. "There's Sónyi's grave," she said at one point, with a vague gesture toward a spot beneath tall trees, but she didn't stop.

After quarter of a mile, we turned westward up a hill. Opapa's grave was beside the path, halfway to the top. A small cross was etched near the top of the headstone. Carved in raised relief under it were his name, "Reich Gusztáv," and below it, the years of his life: "1879–1949." Irregular blotches of white marred the concrete surface, as though someone had tried to clean it but abandoned the project. The wind had risen during our stroll and Leon shielded the match I used to try to light the candle. Several matches later, the flame finally caught. I placed the candle on the crypt in front of a nosegay of white flowers from an unknown donor. The three of us stood at the foot of the grave and bowed our heads. "Végre itt vagyok, Opapa" (I'm finally here), I whispered to my grandfather.

I recalled how the Communists had stripped him of all he had worked for, as well as his tragic and untimely death, allegedly at their hands. When my father described to me how Opapa had defied the Communists to the end, I began to imagine that his tenacity lived on in me—that it was his tenacity that had enabled me to advocate for abused and neglected children as a social worker; to lead my chaos-ridden child welfare agency to stability as its interim executive director; to give solace to critically ill cancer patients as a volunteer; to pursue a career as a writer. I began to see my grandfather as a flesh-and-blood human being, someone who inspired me, someone I loved.

Looking down at his grave, I began not only to cry, but to sob. As Marinka later wrote my parents, it was all Leon could do to console me. In the city where our lives had intersected for just two months in that house on Dózsa György utca a lifetime ago, standing at Opapa's grave would be the closest I would ever get to him. I grieved.

I still felt shaky as we left the cemetery and headed toward the former Reich house and factory. "I can't wait to show you where you lived," Marinka said. I didn't have the heart to tell her Leon and I had already been there twice before. Our second visit had only increased my desire to get into the house. We had stationed ourselves in front of it, hoping to waylay one of its residents coming or going; we had again peered in the windows of the door for signs of life; we again tried to move the handle—all in vain. Marinka may have wondered at my lack of emotion, and I hoped she would attribute it to my being spent from the scene at Opapa's grave.

"I'd like to try to get inside," I told her. She took us into the school next door, only to find that the buildings were not connected. Spending more time at the house and later driving by the former factory's second location, I again thought of the papers my father wanted. "Do you think the library across from your apartment would have documents about the factory?" I asked Marinka.

"They might. Let's go there later and find out," she said.

We had lunch at the Gödör, a cave-like restaurant below street level, its tables covered with red-and-white checked tablecloths. Marinka, who only then revealed that she suffered from glaucoma, could barely see in the dim light. Leon and I, each holding one of her arms, guided her to our table. Over goulash and noodles, we talked more about the past.

"Your father and Sónyi and Imre loved boating on the Rába River," she said. "They were such great friends."

I enjoyed hearing about my father's adventures on the water when he was young. In the United States, his struggles to provide for his family and my mother's aversion to boats transformed him into an armchair sailor.

"Were you the baby your mother was carrying the day she escaped?" Marinka asked me.

"Yes, I was," I said. Had she seen my mother carrying me that last day, or only heard about it? Regardless, it seemed fitting that a person with a connection to that event was welcoming me on my first trip back to my birthplace.

"The sergeant who smuggled you to Austria was a classmate of mine," she said.

"Really?" I asked.

"His name was Györök Matyi," Marinka said. The name was one my parents had long forgotten, a name I could now attach to the man who saved us from forty years behind the Iron Curtain.

After lunch, we stopped at the library. As a library lover since childhood, I was pleased to see that Szombathely's was modern and spacious, with neatly arranged shelves. There were few patrons, perhaps because it was a weekday. We found the documents section on the third floor, but I hesitated to approach a librarian, unsure of the protocol. How would a request for information about a firm predating Communism be received? Would I be viewed with suspicion? Yet again, my parents' fear and distrust shadowed me. Marinka, sensing my reluctance, took charge. "Do you have any information about the Reich Gépgyár from 1948 backward?" she asked the dark-haired librarian. The woman was young, so young that she had probably spent little of her life under Communism. And volunteering at the Seattle Public Library had taught me that librarians' business is information, that they make no judgments about the type of information sought or the person seeking it. Surely it was the same in a free Hungary. Still, I was grateful for Marinka's help and even more grateful when the librarian identified several relevant documents in an index. I asked for copies of all of them.

When we dropped Marinka off at her apartment, she insisted we take the leftover cookies from that morning wrapped in a box, and she also gave us bottles of cherry liqueur and Tokay wine that she had bought as gifts for my parents. "We'll be in touch before we leave town," I promised her.

* * *

That evening in our hotel room, I studied the documents from the library. The Reich Gépgyár was now not just part of our family lore, but of objective reality, of history. From a Szombathely album commemorating the city from 1777 to 1927, an item about Opapa starting the factory in 1920. A display ad from the 1930s about the factory's products:

turbines, machinery for brickworks and textile factories, and tractors. An article about the aftermath of the factory takeover, when the Reich name was stripped from the factory and it became known as the Mezőgazdasági Nemzeti Vállalat (National Agricultural Company). An article from the local newspaper, *Vasmegye*, dated July 16, 1948, a month after our escape, titled, "Uniting the Reich Gépgyár's Two Plants." The article led with a conversation overheard between two workers at the factory's gate:

"Don't worry, comrade, soon we won't have to run back and forth."

"I know. The factory's two sites are consolidating, but it irritates me that the greedy people who ran it before didn't think of this solution. But how could they have? All they cared about was making a profit."

I flinched at the insult to my father and Opapa. But curiosity forced me to read on. Ihász József, the former shop steward and the factory's new manager, was quoted as saying that the entire operation was moving to the factory's second site to cut expenses and increase production by 32 percent. A five-month plan to accomplish those goals was described, followed by a quote from another employee: "We'll stop using certain machines." The speaker's name leaped from the page: Sónyi János. Marinka's husband. The article identified him as the factory's new üzemvezető, deputy, second-in-command—my father's job before the takeover. From the time of our escape until his death in 1983, Sónyi had exchanged letters with my father. Never in all that time had he revealed that he'd ended up with my father's job. I skimmed the rest of the article, about the grandiose plans of the new management, about how everything had improved at the factory with the departure of the Reichs. Finally, I tossed it aside, disgusted.

"I can't believe this," I said to Leon.

"What?" he asked, putting down his book. I told him what I had just read, including the news about Sónyi.

"What do you think it means?" he asked.

"I'm not sure, but if Sónyi had nothing to hide, why didn't he ever tell Dad?"

"Do you think he was collaborating with the Communists before the takeover?"

"I wonder," I said.

"He might just have been in the right place at the right time," Leon suggested. "Or done what he needed to do to survive."

"Maybe. But Sónyi wasn't qualified for that job. He never went to college. He wasn't an engineer," I said, my voice rising with anger.

"Maybe he *was* up to something, then."

"The Communists rewarded people who actively supported them, not bystanders," I pointed out. Leon and I looked at each other, and I confronted the very real possibility that my father's best friend had betrayed him and Opapa. My mother, who told me she had never liked Sónyi and felt uncomfortable around him, would probably not be surprised. But how could I show the article to my father?

Leon went back to his book and my thoughts turned to Marinka. If Sónyi *had* been in collusion with the Communists, had she known? Was that why she was so willing to tend Opapa's grave after all these years, why she wanted to entertain us while we were in town? Perhaps she was motivated less by gratitude than by guilt. What had it been like for her and Sónyi to build a new life on the rubble of my family's misfortune? There were no answers, of course. Four decades had passed since the factory's influence in Szombathely waned with the move of its major operations to Mosonmagyaróvár in the 1960s. It was seventeen years since the fall of Communism, when my father and his nephews, Aunt Marianne's heirs, finally received restitution for the factory, though at a fraction of its value at the time of the takeover.

Marinka may not have known the full extent of her husband's activities at work. And even if she had, her influence on what he did might have been limited. Wasn't her behavior in the present more important than what she had or hadn't done nearly sixty years ago? I wasn't sure. Still, given my questions, I decided I would show my father the article. He deserved to know the facts and draw his own conclusions.

The next day, Leon and I remembered we couldn't take liquids aboard a plane. We would need to return Marinka's gifts. Back at her apartment, Leon waited in the car as I knocked on her door. Her smile of greeting turned to a look of surprise when she spotted the bottles of liqueur and wine I was holding. "We can't take these after all," I told her. "The airline won't let us carry them on."

"But I selected them with such love," she protested, as she took the bottles from me.

"It was very thoughtful of you," I said. "But I'd rather return them to you than have them confiscated at the airport." Still, I felt guilty. Would it have been better to let her think my parents received the gifts even if they didn't? Maybe Hungarian etiquette dictated less than total honesty in a situation like this.

As our stay was winding down, I remembered the money I needed to give Marinka to buy flowers for Opapa's grave. A final visit. She answered the door wearing a blue flowered apron. After inviting me in, she returned to the kitchen to stir a pot of soup simmering on the stove.

"This is for the flowers, plus a small gift from Leon and me," I said, handing her an envelope with 10,500 forints, about $50, in it. The extra money was our way of thanking her for her hospitality, her good intentions toward my parents, her understanding about our not being able to deliver her gift.

"Thank you," she said simply.

I hugged her. Leon and I were leaving the next day, and I knew I wouldn't see her again. Marinka didn't know that in the midst of her kindness, she had inadvertently revealed to me her husband's treachery, and also raised doubts in my mind about her. Gratitude couldn't overcome my indignation. To me, this once-promising relationship was coming to a bittersweet end.

chapter seventeen

In My Mother's Village

A COUPLE OF days after we arrived in Szombathely, Leon and I set off for a day trip to Vasvár, twelve miles to the southeast. I wanted to see the town where my mother was born and spent her childhood, and where Judy's birth father, János, still lived. We also needed to fulfill a request my mother had made.

"Buy some flowers and put them on the grave of Amália Feszta Mozsolics," she'd instructed me after she and my father woke us up with a phone call early in the morning while we were still in Budapest. The woman had been her family's landlord and friend, and Nagymama had worked for her husband as a legal secretary. The bouquet was to be red, white, and green, like the Hungarian flag, and I should have the florist tie a ribbon around it and inscribe it with her and my aunt's names: Vilmy and Évi.

"Where's the grave?" I'd asked, yawning, as I scribbled notes on a pad of paper.

"Near the cemetery chapel," she'd said. "You shouldn't have any trouble finding it."

"We'll do what we can," I'd promised. Still, her asking me

to put flowers on the grave of a woman who wasn't a relative, someone she had rarely mentioned to me, struck me as odd.

The narrow, two-lane road to Vasvár led through a few placid hamlets of stucco houses and was flanked by the same corn and sunflower fields and stands of leafy trees just turning gold that we had seen elsewhere in the area. The day was mild, the weather sunny. I was content to maintain the speed limit of sixty kilometers, or thirty-seven miles, per hour. But impatient drivers on a road busier than we expected quickly overtook us, riding our bumper before they raced past, sometimes even when a car was coming from the other direction. After seeing several close calls, we were relieved to arrive at the turnoff to our destination.

I was surprised to see a steep hill looming ahead of us, with a spire jutting upward from a red-roofed church at its top. My mother had never mentioned that her hometown was built on a hill. This area of Hungary is mostly flat, so I'd assumed that Vasvár was on level land. A small detail, but one that forced me to revise my picture of my mother as a child to someone walking up and down hills, to someone living life on a more vertical plane. Perhaps it was those childhood experiences, followed by living in the foothills of the Alps in Austria after our escape, that led to her love for the mountains of Montana.

In fact, I knew little about Vasvár. Szombathely, as my birthplace and the scene of the events surrounding our escape, was of greater interest to me. But my mother had also nudged me in that direction. Soon after I began my quest to explore my family's past in 2003, Judy and I had been visiting our parents in Billings at the same time. As we chatted at the dining room table, my mother brought out files with newspaper articles, brochures, and photographs she had collected about both towns. Without comment, she handed all the material about Szombathely to me, and everything about Vasvár to Judy. Her doing so made sense, since my research centered on my birthplace, and Judy had spent her early childhood in Vasvár. Yet wasn't it also important for me to know about my mother's hometown, and for Judy to know about the town where we lived with my father's parents before our escape?

Perhaps my mother was trying to compensate Judy for her unwillingness, after revealing that János was her birth father, to discuss him again. She didn't know then that, with my help, Judy had already contacted him. Maybe she hoped that information about the town where he lived would assuage any desire on her part to know more. Whatever her reasons, my mother's actions reinforced for me my lifelong sense that we were a family divided: my mother and Judy, my father and me. It was a pattern, a way of operating so firmly entrenched that it never occurred to Judy and me to copy the materials our mother had given us and exchange them. My sister and I embodied two parts of our family, represented by two towns: Szombathely and Vasvár. Only as Leon and I prepared to travel to Hungary three years later did my mother give me a photograph of her former home and a few basic facts about the town.

I drove up the hill to Vasvár's main square, its centerpiece the salmon-colored Catholic church we had seen from below. Surrounding it were two- and three-story apartment buildings, some painted deep shades of pink or green instead of the usual pastels, with retail businesses—a variety store, a photo shop, a tavern—at street level. Red flowers and greenery filled window boxes on some of the buildings. A handful of people strolled on pavement arranged in a decorative checkerboard design. We were curious to see what else the town of five thousand people had to offer and kept driving, but within minutes we found ourselves once again in the countryside. I turned the car around and drove back to the center.

We had no map and there was no sign of a tourist information office. Our best option seemed to be to orient ourselves on foot. I parked in an open spot on the first street above the main square, lined with buildings abutting each other. I got out of the car and faced a well-kept, two-story aqua building with white and dark green trim around the windows. "That looks like the house where Mom and her family lived!" I exclaimed to Leon. I dug in my purse and pulled out the black-and-white photograph she'd given me. This building shared all the architectural details of the one in the picture: a small, semicircular balcony on the second floor with an ornate wrought-iron railing; a bay window over the double doors of the *kapu,* the gate to the property; a bell-shaped parapet over the window of an attic room. Without a doubt, this was the house where Nagymama and Nagypapa had raised my mother and Aunt Évi on the first floor and where their landlords, the Mozsolicses, had lived above them. Vasvár, though small, had plenty of other streets and houses. What cosmic forces had led us to an open parking space directly in front of the house I was seeking? Our ending up there without effort seemed to validate my desire to learn as much as possible about my mother's life in this place.

The gate was open. Feeling bolder than we had been at my cousin Suzie's former home in Szombathely, Leon and

I stepped through it into a wide tunnel. To our left was the entrance to the house, double doors with peeling white paint and a concrete stoop indented from the footsteps of the many people who had crossed it over the years. I imagined that the footsteps of my mother, my aunt, and my grandparents had contributed to the wear and felt a link to their long-ago selves. At the end of the tunnel was the backyard, a jungle of deciduous trees and shrubs encroaching on a compact area filled with weeds. The space looked nothing like the inviting grassy expanse my mother had described to me, where she and Aunt Évi spent hours playing with their friends on warm summer days. On the rare occasions when she mentioned her childhood home, my mother said that she wanted to draw a picture of what the yard looked like then. She had an artistic flair that manifested itself in her sewing and knitting projects and the tasteful way she decorated our house on a limited budget, but she also seemed intrigued by the idea of expressing herself through drawing. Sadly, among the many obligations of her life, she never took the opportunity. The picture of the yard as it was then remained only in her imagination.

On my bookcase at home is a sepia-toned photograph from that time, of my mother, perhaps ten years old, and Aunt Évi, eight, with Nagypapa. Despite the family's modest means, Nagymama insisted on dressing her daughters well, to the envy of their friends. The sisters sit on either side of their father, clad in matching sailor dresses that I imagine as navy blue with large white collars and red bows tied in front. Nagypapa gazes into the distance under his chauffeur's hat; Aunt Évi looks directly into the camera with a serious expression. My mother, her short blonde hair parted on one side, leans her head against his shoulder and looks past the camera with an enigmatic half-smile, a hint of her inclination to keep her deepest feelings to herself. Still, I know from her that she adored her father, and that her relationships with her mother and sister were more complicated.

Looking at the crumbling gray stucco and mismatched windows on the back of her former home, I longed to know more about the girl in that sailor dress—what she was like, what she thought about, what had happened to her within those walls. I hadn't always been so interested and doubted if I had ever asked my mother to tell me about her childhood in any detail. As with so many aspects of the past, I had detected her reluctance to reveal information and tended to settle only for what she offered. She did tell me she had been lonely as a child, but didn't elaborate. She loved playing with a porcelain doll, and she had been overjoyed to receive an orange for Christmas during the Great Depression.

How had her simple joy at receiving that gift as a child transformed into more complex feelings when it came to Christmas with her own children? I remembered one Christmas Eve when I was twelve or thirteen. I found her in the basement of our house on Avenue B, wrapping gifts that would be opened that night. As we had in Europe, we still celebrated Christmas on Christmas Eve, rather than Christmas morning, as most people in Billings did. One more way we were different. She was bent forward, her back to me, tying a ribbon around a package on one of the large green wooden trunks that had transported our possessions to America. I hesitated at the foot of the stairs, sensing she wouldn't want me to see what she was doing. Peering into the dimness surrounding the pool of light over her work area, I noticed that her back was shaking. I heard muffled sobs.

"Mom?" I asked, alarmed. My worries about whether she wanted me there forgotten, I rushed to her side. "What's wrong?"

She turned to me, her face streaked with tears. "I feel bad that Dad and I couldn't afford to get you kids many presents this year," she said, wiping her eyes with her apron. "Just a few little things." She gestured toward a small pile of gifts wrapped in red and green paper sitting on the trunk.

"Oh, Mom, I don't mind," I said. I put my hand on her shoulder, hoping my touch would convince her.

"Really?" she asked, her tongue rolling the *r* as her lips curved into a faint smile.

"Really," I answered, my voice firm. I knew my parents were struggling financially, since my father had only recently been hired as a night watchman at Eastern Montana College. The autonomy of that job and a later one as a security guard enforcing parking rules suited him, and he would remain with the college until he retired fifteen years later. But whether my parents could afford them or not, I wasn't preoccupied with Christmas gifts. From an early age, I had been only too aware of the obstacles my parents faced as refugees and did everything I could to avoid adding to them. An echo of my mother's childhood ability to be grateful for what was possible, to not long for more. Still, my nonchalance sometimes backfired.

Another memory, this one a year or two later. "Why aren't you in the Christmas spirit?" my mother demanded of me.

"I don't know," I said. How could I explain my adolescent moodiness? Still, I sang carols as we lit the candles on our Advent wreath; helped decorate the tree with silver ornaments and Hungarian *szalon cukor,* candies wrapped in fringed white tissue and foil; bought and wrapped presents. I tried to conjure up an enthusiasm I didn't feel to please a mother who seemed able to feel joy at Christmas only if I felt it, too, or at least acted like I did.

My mother's former home in Vasvár had no doubt changed in the six decades since she had lived here. But the current appearance of the house, its back as rundown as its façade was immaculate, suggested that tendency of my mother and the rest of my family to favor appearances over messy reality. Given the hardships they had endured, I could understand their attitude toward an outside world that was not always welcoming. After all, I had followed their example when, over the years, I'd tried to hide my Hungarian heritage. But I found it more difficult to accept that attitude when we communicated within our family. I longed for us to share our frustrations, fears, and hurts, and not only when they were discovered by accident. As an adult, I was becoming more open in my life, and I felt more and more frustrated trying to abide by the family rules.

The yard was deserted, and no one seemed to be in the house, either, at least no one who cared that we were trespassing. After looking around and taking some pictures, we retraced our steps through the tunnel to the street.

* * *

Back at the main square, next to the church, Leon and I entered a thirteenth-century building that was now a local history museum. I thought it was the former site of the convent elementary school my mother and Aunt Évi had attended, and imagined my mother carrying her books and laughing with friends in the low-ceilinged arched hallways. The nuns in black robes and white wimples who ran the school and taught the classes had been very strict. When their teacher was speaking, students were required to sit ramrod-straight, their hands clasped behind their backs at near-shoulder level. Misbehavior resulted in slaps on the hand with a ruler. Still, my mother was bright and excelled. She was eager to move on from elementary school when the time came. But Nagymama and Nagypapa worried that Aunt Évi, less accomplished than her older sister, might feel lost without her presence, so they asked the nuns to hold my mother back a year. Separated from her friends, her academic progress hindered, my mother grew resentful, especially toward Nagymama.

Was it that failure to take her needs into account, coupled with impending adolescence, that unleashed her rebellious streak? By the time she was fourteen or fifteen, she strolled the streets where Leon and I now walked, looking at boys and biting her lips to redden them, fluffing her long blonde hair to make herself even more attractive to them than she already was. She and her mother clashed more often over her behavior as she got older.

"What's going on between you and that Kovács boy?" Nagymama might have demanded.

"Nothing," my mother might have responded, sullen.

"People talk about how you flirt with him."

"So what?"

"Have you kissed him?"

"I'd like to."

"You'd better be careful."

"Why?"

"He looks like he wants more than a nice girl should give."

"I can handle him."

"Are you sure? I don't want you to get in trouble."

"Why don't you trust me?"

When my mother and I argued, I sometimes couldn't help thinking that, even when the content differed, we were reading from the same script of mother-daughter discord. As much as I might have wished it otherwise, it was as though the lines were predetermined and couldn't be changed.

By the age of nineteen, my mother was married to an accomplished musician named János and had given birth to Judy. She hinted years later that this was a marriage engineered by Nagymama, perhaps to try to rein her in. It was a loveless marriage, she'd tell me, yet she must have felt some affection for the father of her beloved firstborn child, at least initially. With János away fighting in the Hungarian Army during World War II, she was more single parent than wife. She rode the train to Szombathely five days a week to work at the Reich Gépgyár while her parents cared for Judy. It must have been wrenching for her to leave her baby, but she did what she needed to do for them to survive. When the marriage ended along with the war, she had no regrets. She'd already met my father. János became a forbidden subject.

In Vasvár, knowing that Judy's birth father lived nearby intrigued me. I imagined finding his house at number 34 on a street named for the revered poet Jozsef Attila. Perhaps he would be working in his garden and I would stop to chat and get acquainted. If he hadn't been a secret for half our lives, if we had grown up knowing he was Judy's father, if our mother had told me about him when she finally told Judy, I might not have felt such a strong pull toward this shadowy figure who, even in his absence, had such a profound impact on our family. But information withheld about someone tends to embellish and enlarge them in the minds of others, to the point that they become far more significant than they might have been otherwise. I thought getting acquainted with János might give me a picture of the woman my mother was when she met and married and had a child with him—before she became the mother with whom I had such a complicated relationship. But I didn't know where the street was located, time was running short, and Leon and I had other obligations to fulfill.

* * *

We bought a bouquet of flowers at a florist's on the main street, and I had the clerk inscribe the ribbon as my mother had instructed. In the cemetery at the top of the hill, gale-force winds whipped around us as we searched for the grave. Roaming paths near the chapel and elsewhere, we saw graves of Tóths and Horváths and Szabós and Kovácses, but none for "Mozsolics Amália," as it would be written in Hungarian, surname first. Finally, I asked an elderly woman if she knew where it was, and she pointed me toward a path we hadn't yet tried. The crypt was where she had indicated, the planter on its top filled with red geraniums and zinnias growing amid a tangle of weeds. A black granite plaque on the concrete headstone read, "Mozsolics Amália." But above it was another name, "Mozsolics István." Nagymama's former employer. My mother hadn't mentioned him. Could the grave-mates possibly be husband and wife, given the thirty-four-year age difference between them? I doubted it. But Leon and I were tired of the fierce wind tugging at us from every direction. And how many Mozsolics Amálias could there have been in this small town? Next to the headstone was a vase already filled with water. I thrust our flowers inside, and we left. I had at least tried to fulfill my mother's request, I told myself, but I also felt a nagging sense that I hadn't succeeded. What would her reaction be?

My mother also wanted us to visit Szentkut, the Roman Catholic shrine Magdi had also mentioned. The sacred place was one of her family's favorite destinations on long walks they took dressed in their church finery on warm summer Sunday afternoons. Only after getting instructions from three people—at the cemetery, the museum on the square, and a travel agency that I mistook for a tourist information office—did Leon and I find it, ironically, off the road we had taken into town. I had missed the sign. The shrine was in a peaceful, wooded glade and consisted of a small chapel; a white plaster well, now dry, topped by a cross; and a statue of the Virgin Mary set into a recess covered with ivy. The trees might have been smaller, but otherwise the setting was probably little changed from when my mother, Aunt Évi, and Nagymama and Nagypapa strolled the paths, climbed the hill, rested on wooden benches, prayed in the chapel.

That night, after we returned from Vasvár, I called my parents. I had promised to check in when we arrived in Szombathely two days earlier but had trouble finding an international calling card. Only that morning had I finally located one in a bookstore. "Hello from Szombathely," I said when my father answered the phone.

"Where have you been?" he demanded. "We've been worried about you." He had called the hotel several times, but when he asked for me, the receptionist hung up. With his hearing loss, he may not have realized that they were likely putting him on hold while they rang our room. They tried calling Marinka to see if she could contact us, but her phone number didn't work. Finally, frantic, they asked Aunt Évi to contact Suzie's cousin, Erzsi, who also lived in Szombathely, to ask her to call us. Erzsi had agreed, but we hadn't yet heard from her. I had viewed my occasional phone calls to my parents as a way to give them a vicarious experience of traveling in Hungary. But from the reactions of my father, and my mother when she joined us on an extension, they seemed most concerned about our safety. Still, when I explained the reason for my delay in calling, they seemed mollified.

"We went to Vasvár today," I told my mother.

"How was it?" she asked.

"We put the flowers on the grave in the cemetery, but noticed another name on the headstone, Mozsolics István."

"You put the flowers on the wrong grave!" my mother exclaimed.

"Really?" I said, though I wasn't totally surprised.

"That was the grave of Amália Mozsolics's daughter, who was buried with her father," my mother said. "The daughter was named after her mother, but the mother was Amália *Feszta* Mozsolics." Belatedly, I remembered writing that additional name down during our Budapest phone call on a piece of paper I had since lost. "The mother was divorced from her husband and was buried in another location."

"Well, where was her grave?" I asked. "We looked everywhere in the cemetery."

"By the chapel," she said, vague as she had been when she'd made her original request. As we talked, I realized that, contrary to what I had assumed, she had never seen the grave herself. She told me Amália Mozsolics, the mother, had died in 1959, eleven years after we left Hungary.

"Look, we did the best we could. It was really windy, there were lots of graves, and we wouldn't even have found this grave if I hadn't asked someone."

"You should have found it," my mother insisted. When she and Aunt Évi were children, they could walk up the hill directly to the front of the chapel. She seemed convinced that the grave was in that location, despite the fact that, at best, her information was secondhand from Uncle Laci, who might have visited the grave on one of his several visits to Hungary.

"But the cemetery entrance is now on the other side, and after all these years there are lots more graves," I said.

"It's okay," my mother responded, though her tone indicated otherwise.

"Why can't you be grateful for what Leon and I tried to do?" I asked, my voice rising.

"Because I wanted the flowers on the mother's grave! I don't care about the daughter!" my mother shouted.

"If we could have found it, we would have. You're not being reasonable."

A pause. "And you're not doing what I think you should do on this trip."

"What?" The sudden shift in our conversation caught me off guard. Changing the subject from the topic at hand was a tactic my mother often used during an argument.

"I could have planned things better for you."

"Oh, really?" I said, unable to hide my sarcasm.

At the other end, a loud *click.* My mother had hung up on me. Tears of rage sprang to my eyes.

"Keep calm," Leon advised.

"The nerve of her," I fumed. "To think that she could have planned our trip better." I knew what I wanted to see, and it didn't necessarily mesh with my mother's ideas. Still, I didn't want an argument with her to poison the rest of our time in Hungary. I took a few deep breaths, swallowed my pride, and called her back.

"Look, Mom, I'm sorry. We did the best we could."

"It's okay," she said. This time, at least, she sounded like she meant it.

My mother's initial reaction made it clear that honoring her family's landlord and friend was more important to her than I realized. But I couldn't escape the feeling that she had also devised the challenging errand to distract me from trying to find János and learning his secrets—secrets she hoped to keep buried in her hometown.

Later that evening, I called Erzsi, with whom I had exchanged a few letters as a child, to let her know we were fine and that I had talked with my parents.

We met with her and her daughter, Andi, for lunch later that week. Leon begged off to take a break from more Hungarian conversations he couldn't understand, and they took me on a tour of Szombathely. Knowing that Erzsi had grown up in Vasvár, and that Andi lived there, I mentioned our putting the flowers on the wrong Mozsolics grave in the cemetery.

They laughed. "It's easy to get mixed up in that crowded place," Erzsi said.

"Do you know where the mother is buried?" I asked.

"I can find out," Andi said. "Buy more flowers and I'll put them on the right grave."

We stopped at a flower shop, and I selected a pot of purple chrysanthemums that would keep better than cut flowers and be less likely to blow away in the wind. The clerk wrapped the pot in green foil, inscribed "Vilmy" and "Évi" on a white ribbon, and tied it around the pot. Amid goodbyes and my profuse thank-yous, Andi promised to put the pot on the grave the next day. She later sent me a photograph of the flowers in front of a black granite headstone inscribed "Mozsolics Amália Feszta." I sent it to my mother, with love.

chapter eighteen

Echoes of the Escape

THE WEATHER DURING most of our trip had been mild and sunny, but on the day Leon and I set out to retrace the route of my family's escape, it rained. Drops coursed like teardrops down the windows of our compact car as we drove through the neighborhood of the former Reich house and factory with their memories of my family's past. We were headed toward the Nárai Road that would take us the ten miles to Austria, the same road my father and Judy, and then my mother, carrying me, traveled those two days in 1948. The dreary damp was a fitting tribute to that pair of long-ago journeys, laced not only with fear, but with sadness, with unshed tears. Beyond St. Stephen's Park, with its modern concrete monument to its namesake, we found the road climbing out of town over the Alsó Hegy, or Lower Mountain. To me, having grown up near Montana's Rocky Mountains, it seemed little more than a gentle rise. The narrow two-lane road passed scattered suburban houses and the edge of the cemetery where we had visited Opapa's grave before it wound into the countryside. Cornfields with spent stalks, pastureland, and fallow ground lay among forested areas and windbreaks of oak, ash, birch, and poplar trees.

Only occasionally did we meet a car traveling in the opposite direction on the rain-slicked pavement.

From the moment Leon and I decided to travel to Hungary, I knew I would make this journey. I had traversed this landscape fifty-eight years earlier, but as an infant, with little awareness of the world beyond the protective circle of my mother's arms. By retracing the path my parents, and especially my mother, took, I hoped to see what I had missed, to get at least a taste of what it had been like for them to cross from one life to another.

Splatters of rain coated the windshield amid the steady *whap* of the wipers. I tried to imagine the scene in the sunny glare of early summer, my father and Judy on a bicycle, my mother gazing out the window of a bus. The corn stalks would have been pale green, their tops close to the ground, containing only the promise of the bounty to follow, not unlike my parents' hopes for a brighter future. The trees, only recently leafed out, would have been younger, the groves less dense. But nature, its cycles largely unperturbed by human activity, would have presented at least an approximation of the scene unfolding before us.

Halfway to the border, we passed through Nárai, little more than a few houses and a couple of inns. Beyond it, tall trees lining both sides of the road arched overhead, creating a dripping tunnel that underscored the day's melancholy mood. The road soon slanted downward into Pornóapáti. This was the town the sergeant had detoured with my father and Judy before guiding them across in a less populated area; where he and my mother had disembarked from the bus. It looked bigger than the cluster of wretched houses my mother had described to me, with several newer buildings and a church painted ocher with white trim, its steeple topped by a verdigris dome and cross. But the atmosphere was eerie. Gated houses, their shutters closed. Streets empty of moving cars, of people. A wisp of pale wood smoke trailing from a chimney was the only sign of human habitation. Which house was the one where the sergeant had led my mother and dropped off the suitcase carrying our family's only possessions? The house with two windows facing the main road, covered in peeling tan paint? The reddish house with a moss-covered roof hunkered behind a larger commercial building? The small house with outsized arched double doors flanked by a stained façade? Perhaps the house no longer existed, its residents long gone, along with our suitcase.

We crossed the shallow gray ripples of the Pinka River on a bridge with metal railings and pressed on in search of the spot where the sergeant had walked my mother across the border. Next to the road, ten or fifteen men, perhaps prisoners, were digging a trench. Their faces and blue uniforms drenched with rain, they stopped and leaned on their shovels to watch us pass. Farther down the road on the opposite side stood the shell of a large two-story building with one-story wings extending on either side of it. Glassless windows stared at the tangle of shrubs and weeds surrounding the structure's pocked and sooty walls. Inside a wrought-iron fence in front, a statue of the Virgin Mary holding the baby Jesus stood on a pedestal, a mass of purple flowers at its base. Was this a former monastery or convent? Perhaps the sergeant and my mother passed this building when it was bustling with activity, the monks or nuns as curious about their motives as the road crew seemed to be about Leon's and mine.

Past the ruin, the road came to an abrupt end at a gate-arm barrier. Leon and I got out of the car and looked into Austria across a frontier filled with tall grasses and shrubs. I pulled out our camera to commemorate the likely spot where my mother and I had left our homeland. Through the viewfinder, I spotted an Austrian soldier in olive-drab fatigues facing us perhaps fifty yards away. A rifle was slung over his shoulder. At his eyes were a pair of binoculars. "That soldier is watching us," I said to Leon.

"I know," he answered. "We should probably get out of here."

I lowered the camera, my picture untaken. Was the man trying to intimidate us? We weren't doing anything wrong, unless taking photographs of the border was still prohibited, as it had been in Austria near the Iron Curtain during our trip in 1979. I figured the soldier was stationed there to prevent people from entering the country without a passport check at an official border station. Leon and I had no intention of trying to sneak across, though it would have been most meaningful for me to cross the border near where my mother and I had. Still, my mouth went dry, and my heart pounded under the soldier's scrutiny. If I reacted that way to a soldier simply doing his job at the border between two free countries, what must my parents have felt in 1948? Then, danger lurked everywhere in this area, though less from Austrian guards than from the soldiers of Hungary's Soviet-backed Communist regime, who stopped at nothing to prevent people from leaving the country.

Did my mother worry about being ambushed by a Hungarian soldier, rifle at the ready, as she and the sergeant walked here? Did she clutch me even closer to her, trying to protect me? Did she ever consider turning back, not taking the risk? The sergeant no doubt told her he had succeeded in getting my father and Judy safely across the border. But she had no way to know what had happened to them in Austria, whether they had avoided Soviet soldiers on the lookout for Hungarian escapees, whether they had arrived safely at a relative's home in Pinkafeld. Courage and hope and the strength of her desire for freedom for herself and her family must have inspired her to keep going, despite any doubts. I had never faced anything remotely resembling such a test. I wondered if I could possibly comprehend what she and my father and Judy had endured, even as I attempted to follow their footsteps.

* * *

Leon and I got in the car and went back the way we had come, past the ruins and the road crew, and over the Pinka River. The closest official border crossing was on Route 89, ten miles to the north. We skirted the border on the way and passed through several villages, each with a compact main square anchored by a Catholic church, and tile-roofed stucco houses squatting in the shadow of Austria's verdant, mist-enshrouded hills to the west. Two stops at the border, one in Hungary and one in Austria, and we were in the province of Burgenland, part of the Soviet-occupied zone in 1948. Austria's prosperity compared to conditions in Hungary was immediately evident from the quality of the road, now Route 63. It was smoother and wider and easier to drive, even in the rain.

Near Grosspetersdorf, the first town after the border,

Leon studied the only map we had brought with us. It was on the back of our Szombathely map and showed a swath of western Hungary, but only a narrow slice of eastern Austria. "This town isn't Oberwart," Leon said, referring to the place that had been pivotal in my mother's escape with me.

"Yes, it is," I said, with the certainty of someone who had pored over that map for months before we arrived in Hungary.

"No, it's not," he insisted. "In Hungarian it's called Nagyszent … ."

"Oh, Nagyszentmihály," I said, suddenly remembering that my father and Judy had spent the night with a relative there after crossing the border. That's all I knew about it. I thought I was coping well with the emotional impact of digging into my family's past, but my confusion suggested otherwise. "I'm sorry, I was wrong," I told Leon.

"Don't worry about it," he answered, smiling. I was filled with gratitude for my husband, who had accompanied me to Hungary mostly to support me in my quest. Without his patience and understanding, the feelings that mingled with my parents' fears and regrets and sadness might have overwhelmed me.

We bypassed Grosspetersdorf and drove on to Oberwart, five miles away. The hour we spent in that town of several thousand emphasized that, for all my pride in my trip-planning skills, I hadn't prepared us for Austria. Had I, in some unconscious way, tried to complicate the trip, to make it impossible for us to breeze through this town where my mother and I had faced such peril from the Soviets? Planning our excursion, I had reasoned that we were only going forty or fifty miles from Szombathely. What I had failed to take into account was that we were going to a different country, with a different language and a different monetary system. We had no map of the town and wound our way up and down several hills before finally locating its center. Everyone spoke German, and the little I remembered of that language soon failed me. Leon and I were reduced to pointing and sign language to communicate at a couple of cafés where we tried to eat lunch. Our credit cards and dollars and forints were useless, since they accepted only euros, in cash. And we couldn't change our money because the banks were closed for two hours in Austria's version of a siesta.

Leon and I turned our attention to the main square, our primary interest. More a wide spot in the street than an actual square, it wasn't the tranquil, almost bucolic space rimmed by a church and houses that I had imagined from what my mother told me. The street teemed with people browsing through piles of clothing and other merchandise on tables set up next to large vans in a mobile market. Busy shops and restaurants lined the square and side streets, many with several stories of apartments above them. There was no sign of the modest, single-family house where the roofer had taken my mother to rest and tend to me before they carried out his plan to get us past the Soviet soldiers and onto the Pinkafeld bus.

Across from the imposing city hall, I noticed a three-story pink building with a wide paved area marked with three lanes in front. The bus station. Somewhere in the vicinity of where Leon and I stood, my mother had lingered and watched the bus parked there. Somewhere close by, she had raced to catch up with the bus as it pulled away, joining Willi, the roofer, aboard. On this pavement now soaked with rain, my mother's courage and her willingness to trust a stranger had secured her future—and mine.

Another five miles took us to Pinkafeld. Similar in size to Oberwart, it was more picturesque, its main street winding up a hill lined with immaculate examples of the pastel-hued Baroque buildings prevalent in the region, in both Hungary and Austria. It was here that my mother and I were reunited with my father and Judy, where my parents finally allowed themselves to believe their dreams of freedom would be realized. I didn't know where we had stayed, so we would once again connect with the past in a cemetery. Omama, Aunt Marianne, and Uncle Zénó were all buried in Omama's family's crypt there. I wanted to honor a grandmother I had known only through letters and the relatives I had met on our trip in 1978 by putting flowers on the grave. This time, it wasn't Marinka who thwarted my plans. A sign on the door of the local flower shop indicated that it was closed until three thirty p.m., an hour-and-a-half later.

I sighed. "There's no point in waiting. Let's go on to Rohrbach and get flowers on the way back," I said. "Hopefully we'll be able to use a credit card."

"Okay, but before we go, let's find the cemetery, to save time later," my ever-practical spouse suggested.

We soon found the cemetery we had visited with my parents in 1978 on top of a hill overlooking the town. People clad in dark clothes were gathering for a funeral in the adjacent church, but no one stopped us from driving through the gates. In an area much smaller than the cemetery where Opapa was buried, I easily found the crypt on the perimeter, a headstone ten feet tall, flanked by Doric columns and topped by a pediment inscribed "Familie

Friedrich," Omama's maiden name. A dozen black plaques engraved in gold covered the front. Aunt Marianne's and Uncle Zénő's names were on a single plaque at the foot of one of the columns. I traced the letters with a heavy heart, regretting that we had met only that one time. As I scanned the headstone looking for Omama's plaque, I heard voices yelling in German behind me. A pale young man dressed in black and a heavyset, middle-aged companion, perhaps cemetery employees, strode toward us among the graves. They motioned that we needed to move our car from the cemetery. Leon went to comply and I soon followed. I would have more time to reflect at the grave when we returned with our flowers.

We couldn't duplicate the path my parents walked, over hills and through forests, to arrive at our new home in Rohrbach. Instead, Leon and I followed the road that the relative who drove Judy and me there probably took. Our map ended at Pinkafeld, forcing us to rely on road signs to guide us.

"There's a sign for Rohrbach," Leon reported a mile or two from Pinkafeld's outskirts.

"Great, we're on the right track," I said. But as we drove on, the town wasn't mentioned again. We stopped at a modern gas station and mini-mart that could have been on any highway in the United States.

"Rohrbach an der Lafnitz?" I asked the young female cashier.

"Pinggau," she answered, which we understood to mean that, to get to our destination, we should head toward a town by that name that *was* mentioned on road signs. It was just as well that she didn't say more since I likely wouldn't have understood her.

We were traveling through the eastern foothills of the Alps, dotted with quaint towns among deciduous trees. All were spotless, their buildings carefully painted, with no sign of litter or graffiti. But they also struck me as slightly sterile, even cold. I found myself thinking fondly of Hungary's messiness.

Past Pinggau, we turned toward Graz, where my parents shopped when we lived in Rohrbach. We drove several miles, but not only was there no sign of Rohrbach, there was no sign of any town, in an area where there seemed to be a town every few miles.

"This can't be the right way," Leon said.

"We should have gotten there by now," I agreed. We turned around and headed back in the direction we had come. Soon signs appeared for Vienna, seventy-five miles to the north. The wrong way.

After stopping twice more for directions, we ended up back on the road we had been on before. We hadn't gone far enough the first time. Our zigzagging by car didn't begin to compare with my parents' hours-long, dangerous slog on foot. Still, why should we get to Rohrbach without effort, when it had been so arduous for them?

* * *

A road curved down from the highway into Rohrbach's narrow valley. The main street, the most likely site of the places I remembered, was on the town's near edge. Driving its length, I saw nothing familiar—not my great-aunt Dóra's grand two-story white house or the lumber mill managed by her husband, Kálmán, where my father worked, or Mausburg, the apartment building where we lived. In their place were newer businesses: a gas station, a lumber company, a tire store. We turned off onto twisted side streets lined with more modest versions of Aunt Dóra's house. We must have walked these streets, my mother pushing Robie's baby carriage. Had we ever stopped at the small white chapel to rest on the bench in front? I didn't know. Rohrbach might have been any town, not one where we had lived for more than three years.

The road we were on led to a rise, giving a broader perspective of the valley and surrounding green hills. "Oh, look, there's the railroad trestle!" I exclaimed to Leon. Finally, a familiar landmark. We drove to it on the outskirts of town, two massive stone pillars supporting three arcs with vertical and diagonal joists curving down from the track.

The trestle is the centerpiece of a treasured family photograph my father took while we lived in Rohrbach. My parents had the original black-and-white snapshot enlarged and framed, and they hung it among other family photographs on their bedroom wall. Judy, a tiny figure in a dark coat, stands on a road under the trestle. Next to her is a wooden wagon in which Robie and I sit facing each other. Only the back of his head is visible. The photograph gives no hint of the trials to come. We're just enjoying an outing on a sunny day.

"I wish we had stayed in Rohrbach," my mother sometimes said to me. I didn't know how to respond. I couldn't imagine trading the comfort and familiarity of my life for an unknown. Still, how could I blame her for second-guessing the decisions she and my father made, given the many challenges they faced as refugees in Billings? A natural reaction to broken dreams.

What would our lives have been like if we had stayed? As

children, we could have adapted anywhere; Judy and I were already learning to speak German. My parents would have had an easier time in a country whose language my father spoke fluently, a country that while not entirely familiar, was much closer to their homeland and the people they loved than Billings, Montana. My father's job at the lumber mill owned by Omama and her siblings provided a measure of financial security and status. He chafed under the authority of Kálmán, his overbearing boss, but he might have eventually found a more satisfying position elsewhere in the family enterprises. My parents might have been able to afford specialized care for Robie to enable him to stay at home with us. After the 1956 Revolution, our family would have been reunited with Omama and Aunt Marianne and Uncle Zénó in Eisenstadt, an hour away, and the relatives who had joined us in Billings likely would have remained in Austria if we were there. They certainly would not have gone to Billings, as unfamiliar to them as it had at first been to us. And even if my parents ultimately decided to emigrate to the United States, it might have been easier after the Revolution, when refugees from Hungary were hailed as freedom fighters who took on the Soviets instead of refugees from a country defeated by the Allies in World War II.

I wanted Leon to photograph me in the same spot where I sat in the wagon in that iconic piece of my family's history. But the traffic on the road was heavy, and I had to settle for a picture of the gap between dark green hills spanned by the imposing structure. On the way back to town, we took a side road to the banks of the Lafnitz River. The waterway of my earliest memories had been wide and deep enough in the center to float a large log Judy and I rode on as my parents pushed it between them. What we saw was a narrow creek barely deep enough for wading. Still, given how strange the rest of Rohrbach seemed to me, I was grateful for these tangible links to the time our family spent there.

The rain abated as we drove back toward Pinkafeld, but the sky looked unusually dark. "Do you still want to stop?" Leon asked.

"Yes," I answered. Our visit to the cemetery felt incomplete without leaving flowers to mark that we had been there.

It was past three thirty when we returned to the flower shop. The "closed" sign was still out, the shade on the door pulled down. I noticed a woman standing nearby and, with gestures, asked her if there were any other florists in town. She pointed to a street up the hill. We cruised back and forth on that street and several others, but didn't find one.

"What now?" Leon asked.

I was torn. I longed to stay, to spend time near the crypt containing the remains of Omama and my aunt and uncle, but I worried about driving back to Szombathely in the dark.

"We should go," I said, the words catching in my throat. Regret washed over me for not planning our trip better, for not leaving Szombathely earlier, for once again being unable to honor my relatives in the way I had planned.

Driving eastward toward Hungary in the gathering dusk, we reversed the journey that had retraced my family's steps into a new life. We went back—back to where my family began, back to where our lives changed, back to the repository of our past—to a country that I was also starting to envision as a significant part of my future.

chapter nineteen

Full Circle

WITH JUST ONE day left in Szombathely, I wanted to make one last visit to our former home. It didn't matter that we had already been there three times; the house drew me like a magnet. At five o'clock on a Friday afternoon, Leon and I again stood on the narrow blacktop sidewalk in front. I longed to wash the graffiti off the house, to peel away the chipping paint, to peer beyond the crumbling stucco of its formidable façade, to move even closer to my family's past.

I've long felt drawn to houses where I once lived, as though by being near them—and, if I'm lucky, walking through their rooms—I can recover the essence of the person I was when I lived there. Several years before our Hungary trip, I took a jaunt to the mid-century modern house near Lake Washington in Seattle where Leon and I spent the first years of our marriage. I turned onto Fifty-fifth Avenue South and parked in front of the house on its rise several feet above the street. Before long, Randy, the unmarried air traffic controller who had bought it from us fourteen years earlier, pulled up behind me in his truck. I got out to talk to him. "Could I go in and see the living room drapes?" I asked him, explaining that I wanted to try to find similar window coverings for a current bedroom remodeling project.

"No problem," he said, before leading me up the curved pathway in a front yard filled with Mugho pines, rhododendrons, a Japanese laceleaf maple, a birch tree. The house was no longer sage green, as it had been in our time. Leon and I had spent every free weekend one summer painting the siding to blend into the surrounding landscape. Now the house was white, stark against the greenery. We entered the house through a door once dark olive, now bright fuchsia.

After I inspected the drapes, Randy allowed me to linger in our former home—in the living room with its floor-to-ceiling windows and Roman brick fireplace where Leon and I had entertained family and friends; in the adjoining dining space, where we ate meals at a round teak table and shared news, solved problems, made plans; in the kitchen beyond, separated from the dining room by a peninsula, where, through trial and more than a few errors, I learned to cook. For a few precious moments, I was once again that young bride, filled with a sense of anticipation, of possibility, of choices yet to be made at the start of her married life.

But what was I looking for in the house on Dózsa György utca in Szombathely? When my mother had carried me from there for the last time, I was only two months old. What imprint could I possibly have left? Perhaps it was my parents I was hoping to glimpse as they had been while living here, an exuberant newly married couple with the same sense of anticipation I had felt. I could get a sense of the carefree people they had been before hardship transformed them into the more complicated parents I knew. But it was also nostalgia—not mine, but theirs—that drove me to try to get into the house. Their longing for a past that could never be recovered had embedded itself in me. They would never return here, so I could do it for them.

Leon's and my previous visits had yielded no clues as to what was inside the house. In the waning light, it looked as forbidding as ever. No signs of life, no lights burning inside, no shadows stirring behind lace-curtained windows. We stood staring at the still-immobile front door. "I wonder if it's barricaded shut," I said to Leon.

"This can't be the entrance," he said. "Let's go around the corner and see if there's another way to get in."

"Why not?"

Several yards down the side street, a ten-foot-tall wooden gate stood tantalizingly ajar. Leon and I looked at each other and paused only briefly before we tiptoed through it. Inside was a dirt courtyard filled with racks laden with pipes of various shapes and sizes under a corrugated metal roof, the inventory of the sheet metal business. This area had once been the courtyard of the factory's original site. Opapa had bought and built these surrounding structures to expand the factory's operations, and he worked in them until the Communists wrested it all from him thirty years later. My father had spent countless hours as a child and young man in this courtyard and in these buildings, learning the techniques of manufacturing agricultural machines before becoming a mechanical engineer and returning to work alongside his father for sixteen years. And somewhere within these stucco walls, he had also met and fallen in love with a payroll clerk named Vilmy, my mother.

Thrilled that we had gotten this far, I started to take photographs. Here, I didn't care that we were trespassing. But I soon felt Leon's tug on my arm. I lowered my camera to face a heavyset, middle-aged woman with straw-like, dyed blonde hair staring at me with a questioning look. "Én itt születtem" (I was born here), I told her, pointing toward the house. "This is my first time back in fifty-eight years and I'd like some pictures for my family," I continued, still in Hungarian. The woman seemed to understand but didn't respond. She turned and walked back into the building nearest the gate. "I hope we're not in trouble," I murmured to Leon. Was she getting someone who would order us to leave, or calling the police?

The woman reappeared a few minutes later with a stocky man near her age wearing a red sweater, apparently her husband. To my relief, he was smiling and seemed willing to listen. I repeated what I had told his wife.

He was silent for a moment. "Ismerik a Reichékat?" (Do you know the Reichs?) he finally asked me.

Was it possible that he knew of my family? In my initial excitement, I thought he had been personally acquainted with my grandparents. But of course, he was too young. "Gusztáv Reich was my grandfather," I answered, as proud as I had ever felt in my life.

"In that case, please come in," the man said, motioning us to follow him. Even stronger evidence than Marinka's that, in spite of the events of 1948, people in Szombathely had held my family in high esteem. Thanks to our persistence and timing and the kindness of these strangers, I was finally going to see the house where I was born.

The man introduced himself and his wife as Mr. and Mrs. Horváth, a common surname in Hungary shared by my cousin Suzie's family. Mrs. Horváth excused herself to do some paperwork as her husband prepared to give us a tour.

We followed him to the front of the house, through the stale, musty air of several sparsely furnished rooms, their windows firmly shut, followed by a short hallway. The Horváths seemed to be using the house as a combination office and pied-à-terre, rather than as their primary residence. What had once been the foyer of the house had become a storage area whose contents included a fire extinguisher, a battered radiator, a large cabinet, and copper pipes set on racks and leaning against a wall and a staircase to an attic. Mr. Horváth confirmed that the door Leon and I had tried in vain to open was indeed bolted shut, to try to discourage thieves who preyed on them regularly. "We're God-fearing people," he said. "But we don't know what else we can do to defend ourselves. Crime in this town is getting worse all the time."

"Sajnálom" (I'm sorry), I said. The plight of a couple who worked hard and only wanted to protect their possessions moved me. But I was also sad that our former home had, of necessity, become a fortress. A few days earlier, I had been shocked to read in *Vas Népe* (People of Vas County), the newspaper for Szombathely and the surrounding area, that an elderly shop owner had been robbed and stabbed to death early one afternoon on the next street over from where Suzie's cousin Erzsi lived. No one was talking and there were no suspects. The Horváths' fears and frustrations were apparently well-founded. Hungary's freedom after Communism had brought with it other dangers.

We followed Mr. Horváth back into the house on battered concrete stairs through a doorway narrower than the wide, stately entrance my mother had described on the floor plan she drew for me. I had studied that diagram until I knew the layout of the house as well as I knew my own. In the hallway beyond the door, my mental picture of the floor plan clicked into place, and I began to identify what the rooms I was seeing had been when we lived there. To our right was the former guest bedroom that Opapa had used as an office in the early days of the factory. Now, it contained piles of boxes, odd pieces of wooden furniture, cases of bottled water. On the other side was the former kitchen, empty except for a bare wooden coat tree.

Straight ahead was the dining room, where my parents and grandparents and Judy, when she wasn't visiting Nagymama and Nagypapa in Vasvár, ate their meals at a mahogany table covered with damask. I, too, would have been present at some of those family gatherings, perhaps in the arms of my mother or father, amid conversations increasingly dominated by the question of escape. Standing in the space, I looked beyond the twin bed on a high platform in the center, the small table with a globe on it in one corner, the stained patch of the wooden floor where the finish had worn away. I imagined my parents at the table in the first weeks and months of their marriage, smiling at each other and flirting under the indulgent gaze of my grandparents. Did a part of them—a few atoms or molecules of their joy at finding each other, of their hopes for the future—linger in this room with its drab white walls?

Beyond the dining room was the former salon, its floor covered with a loosely woven green-and-blue-striped area rug. Tables and chairs lined its walls and in the corner of the room stood an upright vacuum cleaner. As they had in 1948, lace-curtained windows looked onto a tree-lined street, though the building housing a kindergarten opposite the house was gone, replaced by an open space enclosed by a wrought-iron fence. Omama had relaxed on a gray velvet sofa here and read books like *Contessa Kate,* one of her favorites. Perhaps she drank tea from a porcelain cup as she perused a book that might have been a 1940s version of a romance novel, or a piece of light historical fiction. Just as she had indulged herself with an occasional cigarette when meeting with other engineers' wives at the Palace Café, she might have sought respite from her duties running the household with a book that was pure entertainment.

A door from the salon led to her and Opapa's former bedroom. There, a large desk littered with papers, two tall bookshelves, and a wall clock suggested that the Horváths used the room as an office. Walking through the house, I had started to feel the all-too-familiar lump forming in my throat. It was in this room, on February 12, 1949, that my sixty-eight-year-old grandfather lay in his bed with a fever. A nurse from his doctor's office walked in, pulled a syringe from her bag, and plunged it in his arm. Within moments, he was dead. Eleven months after the factory takeover, the Communists were consolidating their stranglehold on the country. No autopsy had been performed. These walls held the answer to the question of whether Opapa was killed by accident or murdered by the Communists.

And finally, my parents' former bedroom. The Horváths had transformed it into a parquet-floored kitchen, with a small stove and refrigerator, a glass-fronted cabinet filled with dishes, and a table covered with a flowered cloth and flanked by two chairs. Then, the room had been furnished with dressers and wardrobes and my parents' two twin beds covered with white linens and red satin down comforters. It was on my mother's bed in this room overlooking the former

Reich Gépgyár that I was born on April 24, 1948. Finally, the tears I had been holding back flowed.

After a lifetime, I had come full circle. And though I hadn't expected it, I felt a tender connection to that infant who entered the world in this room amid her family's darkest moments and became the unwitting reminder of all they had lost.

chapter twenty

Intermezzo

BACK IN BUDAPEST, Leon and I sat in our darkened room at the Hotel Victoria and admired a full moon veiled by thin clouds hanging over the dome of St. Stephen's Basilica. That shining orb illuminating our final night in Hungary seemed to validate my shining a light on a family history once cloaked in darkness. The fiery glow of the sunrise reflected in the smooth, bluish waters of the Danube the next morning underscored my sense that returning to my homeland was one of the wisest decisions I had ever made.

"I hate to leave," I told Leon in the cab on the way to the airport, already homesick for Hungary, for all it had revealed. At the moment our plane lifted off from the runway, one thought consumed me: *For the first time in my life, I am whole.*

Even as our flight headed to Amsterdam amid scattered clouds over green fields, I knew that statement wasn't entirely true. Yes, I felt more grounded than I ever had, with a clearer idea of where I came from, in both a literal and figurative sense. But I left behind unfinished business—places unexplored, relationships unfulfilled, insights not fully formed. Leon and I hadn't had time to visit Lake Balaton and the towns along its shores, including Balatongyörök, where

Omama lived with Aunt Marianne and her family after the Communists evicted her from her home. I had only begun to know Magdi and Erzsi and Andi. János, Judy's birth father, remained a mystery. Leon and I had barely left, and already my homeland was tugging at me to return.

Back home, I sorted our many photographs and put them into albums for us and my parents and Judy and Aunt Évi and Suzie. I also sent my parents a copy of my travel diary and the documents about the Reich Gépgyár I had obtained with Marinka's help at Szombathely's main library. I looked at our albums again and again, taking special pleasure in photographs that showed Leon and me in the places where we had been: the two of us leaning against the railing of the Chain Bridge in the light of the setting sun, Leon smiling behind the bronze statue of James Joyce that seemed to emerge from a wall on Szombathely's main square, me standing in front of the Erika Dress Shop in Vasvár. As the immediacy of our trip faded with the passage of time, those photographs confirmed that we had indeed been in those places. At times, I was seized by an almost-visceral longing to again watch the sunset over Castle Hill in Budapest from an outdoor café by the Danube in Pest, to stroll the main square in Szombathely, to drive through the countryside of corn and sunflower fields to Vasvár. How could a country I had viewed with such indifference for most of my life now exert such a strong pull on me?

But it wasn't just the place; it was also the people: kind strangers and hotel staff members who helped us acclimate; the Horváths, who allowed us into my family's former home; Magdi and Erzsi and Andi. People who, unlike Hungarians I encountered in the United States, were gracious toward me when I spoke my native language after a lifetime away from my homeland. I sent thank-you notes to the hotels and the Horváths shortly after we returned and began to exchange cards and letters with Magdi and Erzsi and Andi, mostly at Christmas and Easter, but occasionally at other times during the year. Leon and I reminisced about the hours we had spent with them, wondered how they were faring in the bad economy, sent flowers or gift baskets or monetary gifts at Christmas. Magdi and I corresponded about politics and the rising careers of her grandsons and her sadness at a life slowing down as she approached eighty. Writing those letters, and, later, emails, after Magdi's grandsons set her up with a computer, spurred me to delve more deeply into the Hungarian language than I ever had. I learned new vocabulary words from my trusted dictionary, and ruminated about how to express myself, arranging and rearranging words on the page until I was satisfied. I tried using a Hungarian keyboard format, but found it was actually easier for me to type the text as I did in English, and then go back and manually insert the proper accent marks on the vowels that required them.

To satisfy my curiosity about what was happening in Hungary in a broader sense, I went online from time to time to read *The Budapest Sun*, an English-language newspaper, and *Vas Népe* in Hungarian. I especially liked reading news of my hometown—about city government and schools and art events and soccer matches and, though it disheartened me, even the crimes referred to by the Horváths. Those articles bridged the six thousand miles that separated me from my birthplace, connecting me to that community.

Four years later, Hungary's hold on me remained as strong as ever. I had to return.

PART IV

Denouement

chapter twenty-one

House of Terror

MAKING OUR TRAVEL plans only took me a couple of months, and in September 2010, Leon and I were back in Budapest. Leaden skies unleashed torrents of rain on the morning after we arrived as Leon and I walked on Andrássy ut, a wide, tree-lined boulevard in the city's center. Approaching No. 60, a forbidding gray Renaissance Revival building, we slowed down. "I'm not sure I want to go in," I told Leon. Gray blinds at the windows obscured the interior, and giant block letter cutouts on overhangs on two sides of the building spelled out the word "terror."

"It's up to you," he said. We huddled near the doorway, rain dripping from our umbrellas.

From World War II onward, just the mention of this address had sparked dread in every Hungarian. It was here that the Arrow Cross, the Nazi party in Hungary during 1944 and 1945, and, afterward, the Soviet-backed Communists, had punished actual or suspected dissidents. The site was now a museum called the House of Terror, created to remind people of the nefarious acts of those regimes.

Do buildings retain remnants of the energy that once inhabited them? The prospect of entering this grim reminder of the darker elements of Hungary's twentieth-century history frightened me. Would the evil perpetrated here somehow rub off on us? Or would spending time here shed more light on what happened to my family?

"Let's do it," I finally said. I had been curious about this sinister place since I learned of it during our previous trip in 2006, but we hadn't had enough time to come.

Leon and I had flown into Budapest the previous afternoon to spend a couple of days in the city before taking the train to Szombathely, where we would spend a week before returning to the capital for another week. Much had changed since our last visit. Hungary's already precarious economic situation had deteriorated further as a result of the global economic crisis. A new right-leaning prime minister, Viktor Orbán, had been elected a few months earlier, and he was striving to resolve the debt-fueled problems created by the former socialist regime. But progress was slow. People were hurting even more than before. On the way from the airport to the Hotel Opera near the Hungarian State Opera House on Andrássy, our driver had pointed out several half-completed construction projects languishing due to lack of funds. Still, as we walked to the museum, we had passed chic shops and restaurants. We had also found three thriving bookstores within a couple of blocks and stopped to browse for English translations of Hungarian works, poetry for Leon and novels for me. But we had also noticed numerous "*Kiadó*" (For Rent) signs in dirt-smudged windows.

Buying our tickets inside the museum, I was heartened to see several groups of schoolchildren. Perhaps if the younger generation learned of the atrocities committed in this building, these horrors would be less likely to be repeated in the future. But do human beings ever learn? Ongoing wars and terrorist acts and torture of prisoners suggest otherwise.

Covering one wall of the atrium lobby were small black-and-white portraits of the people who had been put to death in the building—three thousand of them. They overlooked a massive T-54 Soviet tank, one of many used to crush the *Forradalom*, the 1956 Revolution.

The museum touched on the Nazis, but its primary focus was the Communist regime. One exhibit dealt with the activities of the Secret Police, the ÁVO my parents had feared, and its later incarnation, the ÁVH, equally adept at inducing terror. Another highlighted the Soviet gulags and Hungarian work camps where prisoners were sent for hard labor, including forty thousand banished to the latter between 1945 and 1948, the year we escaped. Farther on, an exhibit addressed the Communist takeover of private property in those years, but most of the information was about confiscated land. To my dismay, little was said about the seizure of businesses like the Reich Gépgyár, actions equally destructive to the lives of the people who owned them. Other exhibits told of the regime's activities after our escape that contributed to the miseries of the relatives we left behind: propaganda and show trials and suppression of religion.

We next took an elevator to the basement. The gloomy setting with concrete walls and floors seemed remote, yet we could hear the traffic sounds on Andrássy utca, just as the prisoners held here would have. Did that reminder of ordinary life just a few feet away intensify their agony? The conventional cells, dark holes with a narrow cot and a small window in the door, were bad enough. But one cell was so narrow that the prisoner occupying it was forced to stand twenty-four hours a day. The ceiling of another was so low that the prisoner inside could only sit. Officials deprived prisoners of food and water and sleep for several days before taking them to a nearby interrogation room, where they tried to extract information and confessions with beatings and torture using electrical instruments. A drain in the floor carried away water used to revive prisoners when they passed out and to wash away blood. Farther on was a small room with a gallows where those prisoners who couldn't be induced to say what the interrogators wanted to hear were executed. I felt a wave of nausea.

The Soviet-backed Communist regime had touted its benefits to the people early on, but soon demonstrated that it was no different from any other any totalitarian government as it tried to control people's minds and thoughts, battered them into acquiescence, snuffed out opposition. Yet, despite the many voices silenced here, Hungary's citizens still rose up against oppression during the 1956 Revolution. How brave they had been against odds that ultimately proved overwhelming.

Next came the Hall of Tears, a dark room filled with pinpoints of light mounted on crosses and Stars of David. The space commemorated all those who had been imprisoned in this building from 1945 to 1967, when the last prisoners were set free. Unlike the Communism practiced in other countries behind the Iron Curtain, Hungary's version under the leadership of János Kádár had by then become looser, more tolerant of dissent.

At the end of the tour were photographs of the perpetrators, including several women. As is often the case, they looked not like monsters, but like ordinary human beings.

Leon and I were shocked to learn that some of them were still alive and had never been brought to justice.

I had never doubted that my parents' fears before our escape were real, that their reasons for leaving all they knew behind were valid. But the House of Terror hammered home to me just how ruthless the Communists had been when dealing with people who didn't fit their mold, who refused to join the party and follow its dictates—people not unlike my parents and Omama and Opapa. If the ÁVO had arrested my parents after the factory takeover, or if they had been caught during our escape, they might have ended up here. Surrounded by concrete evidence of the Communists' brutality, I suddenly had no trouble believing, as my father did, that they had murdered Opapa, that his collapse seconds after his doctor's nurse gave him a shot had been no allergic reaction. Realizing that the evil of this place had in all likelihood reached into my own family left me breathless, without words. I grasped Leon's arm and leaned close to him as we stepped out of the building onto a sidewalk still drenched with rain.

With the images from the House of Terror seared in my mind as we walked back to our hotel, I found the abandoned storefronts on Andrássy ut to be even bleaker than they had seemed earlier. Gloom threatened to overwhelm me.

* * *

"What time are we meeting Magdi?" Leon asked back in our room.

"Three o'clock," I answered. From our exchange of letters since our first meeting in 2006, I had grown even more fond of my mother's cousin. The reminder that we would be seeing her in a couple of hours at the Művész Kávéház, the Artist Coffeehouse, across the street from the Opera, started to nudge me out of my funk. By coincidence, Magdi's older daughter, Kati, and her husband, Walter, who lived in California, were at the tail end of a visit to Budapest and would join us. This trip, I didn't feel the weight of my parents' constant presence in the background. Returning to Hungary was less intense and emotional for me than seeing it for the first time had been. Perhaps sensing that, my parents also seemed calmer about this trip, with less need to be closely involved.

"You're really back!" Magdi had exclaimed when she called me shortly after we arrived.

"We couldn't stay away," I told her. "And we can't wait to see you."

Leon and I strolled into the café at the appointed hour, and Kati rushed up to greet us. Her hazel eyes were warm, her smile wide. Tousled short brown hair framed a pretty face enhanced with a minimal amount of makeup. "Isn't it funny that we both live on the West Coast, yet we had to come all the way to Budapest to meet?" I asked her as we hugged.

"Yes, it is," she agreed, laughing. She spoke English with a slight accent, having learned the language only as an adult when she moved to the United States with her first husband. We followed her to the back of a room steeped in Old-World grandeur—high ceilings trimmed with gilt scrollwork, mirrored walls, crystal chandeliers. Only the flat-screen TV set high on one wall marred the sense that we had stepped into an earlier era. Magdi came running up and we hugged, too. She was past eighty but seemed no less lively than she had been at our first meeting. Walter, in his early seventies, with thinning red hair and a courtly manner, extended his hand to each of us and we shook it.

At the table they had saved for us, we ate pastries and drank coffee and, later, wine. Magdi made a toast. "We're so glad you've come back, and that we could get together with Kati and Walter," she said, smiling. It was Kati's fifty-eighth birthday, so we also toasted to her.

"What did you do today?" Magdi asked me.

"We toured 60 Andrássy ut," I said.

"Why would you go to that place?"

"We wanted to learn more about Hungary's history."

"Hmm," she replied, frowning. I knew from our earlier discussions that Magdi scorned Hungary's Communist past, and perhaps she didn't like being reminded of its darker aspects. Perhaps she also wanted visitors like us to see Hungary only in a positive light. Despite her apparent disapproval, I felt no regret about confronting past evils.

The two men chatted in English about retirement—Leon's earlier that year and Walter's a few months hence—and we three women chattered in Hungarian about the family, including Suzie. I was relieved to finally be able to break my silence about her breast cancer. After she died in 2008, Aunt Évi had no choice but to reveal that she had been ill for a long time.

"Why didn't she tell us Suzie was sick earlier?" Magdi asked.

"I don't know," I answered. How could I explain my family's ongoing reluctance to discuss vital subjects when I didn't understand it myself?

"How long was she sick?" Kati asked.

"Six years. She did well for five of them but suffered a lot during the last one." I turned to Magdi. "I wanted to tell you when we were here last time. The only reason I didn't was because Aunt Évi insisted that I not say anything."

Magdi nodded, but I could tell she was frustrated. Who could blame her? It must have been an incredible shock for her to learn that Suzie had died, when she hadn't even known she was sick. Why did my family members keep secrets from one another? To protect themselves from possible negative reactions from others? To protect someone they didn't think could handle the truth? Regardless, secrets have a way of eventually coming out, as this one had, often harming those who have been kept in the dark. The more I saw this dynamic play out in my family, the more determined I was to be as open as possible in my own life and to continue to seek out the truth.

As close as I was to her, even I had been unprepared for Suzie's death. By the summer of 2008, she had been too ill to take a trip to Las Vegas we had planned to celebrate our sixtieth birthdays. Instead, I visited her at home in Havre. One night, I lingered near her bed before returning to my motel. Suzie, her head bald with just a hint of dark fuzz on top, rested against a pile of pillows. The cancer had spread to her lungs and brain, and she spoke with a guttural voice I couldn't always understand. She studied me with clouded eyes. "Will you give my eulogy?" she asked.

I stared back at her, speechless. I knew she was dying, but I clung to the hope that she hadn't run out of treatments to buy her more time. "I'd be honored," I finally managed to say. "But I hope I won't need to do it for a long time yet." Over the next couple of days, we spent hours snuggled side by side on her double bed next to a bedside table covered with pill bottles and her collection of angel figurines, reminiscing about growing up together in Billings as a couple of starstruck Hungarian refugee kids who longed to end up in Hollywood.

Three weeks later, I stood at a lectern in front of First Lutheran Church in Havre, packed with Suzie's friends, relatives, and elementary school students. On a table nearby were a black-and-white portrait of her, fetching with short, dark hair; a vase of red roses; a program with a photograph of her in a traditional costume like mine at that Hungarian Independence Day celebration when we were children; a gray urn containing her ashes. I began to speak, echoing the themes she and I had discussed during my visit. I talked about how, after Suzie and her family escaped during the 1956 Revolution and joined us in the United States, I had guided her and helped her acclimate, but that after she was diagnosed with cancer, she had taught me how you cope when your life suddenly changes, when you're afraid of what the future holds, when surgery alters your body, when chemotherapy and radiation make you sick and your hair falls out and you're in pain and you want to give up but you don't, because people are counting on you and there are so many more things to experience in life. When I finished, I returned to my seat and Leon put his arm around me. Only then did I break down, face in my hands, my body heaving with sobs.

In the midst of my grief in the weeks and months afterward, I fantasized about returning to Hungary, to where Suzie's life, as well as mine, began. I remembered how she had also longed to travel, not to our homeland, but to Provence. She hadn't shared my fascination with Hungary. Unlike me, she had lived for eight years in our homeland and had memories not only of carefree days as a preschooler, but also of the 1956 Revolution, of almost being shot, of her family's escape. Why would she want to revisit the scenes of those traumatic events? But she had eagerly perused photographs of lavender fields and towns perched on hillsides and winding country roads in a book I gave her about the South of France, as a prelude to seeing them in person. She died before she could fulfill that dream. A powerful reminder to pursue my own dream while there was still time.

Before I met Kati at the café that day in Budapest, I had seen her only in photographs in my mother's albums, on vacation with Walter in places like Hawaii and Rio de Janeiro, and at home in Lake Arrowhead. Yet, as I watched her and listened to the soft cadence of her voice, she seemed familiar, like someone I already knew. How could that be? She laughed, and suddenly I realized what it was. "You remind me of Suzie," I told her. It wasn't so much her appearance that conjured up images of my cousin, though there was a vague resemblance, but her voice inflections, her facial expressions, her mannerisms. In the two hours I spent with Kati that afternoon, it was as though Suzie had by some miracle been reborn. Those echoes of a beloved cousin and friend I still missed only added to my joy at seeing Magdi again and meeting more of her family.

Back in our hotel room, I noticed a flyer someone had thrust into my hands in the public square in front of St. Stephen's Basilica. An organ concert that included some of my favorite music, including Charles Marie Widor's "Toccata" from his Organ Symphony no. 5, was scheduled for that night. Navigating the highs and lows of the day had left me exhausted, but perhaps listening to music I loved would refresh me and help me heal from the House of Terror's darkest moments. "I'd like to go to this," I said to Leon, handing him the flyer.

"Oh, they're playing the 'Toccata,'" he said. "I know how much you love it." My spouse had once scoured Seattle to find me a recording of the piece for my birthday, one of the most thoughtful gifts I had ever received from him. "Of course, let's go."

We had dinner outdoors at a restaurant next to the square and watched people milling around on pavement decorated with multicolored circular designs. Afterward, we joined the crowd walking up a wide staircase under the pediment of the domed neo-Renaissance structure inscribed with the sentence "Ego sum via veritas et vita" (I am the way, the truth, and the life). The high-ceilinged, opulent interior of Budapest's largest church, with room for more than eight thousand worshippers, awed us. Decorating the space were gilt cornices, marble surfaces and sculptures of religious figures, oil paintings of Bible scenes, candelabras, and a huge marble structure on the altar whose centerpiece was a sculpture of St. Stephen.

The musical program included Albinoni's "Adagio" and Gounod's "Ave Maria," and was performed on the Basilica's massive pipe organ, supplemented for various pieces by soprano and tenor soloists, a violinist, and a trumpet player. As I anticipated, the highlight for me was the "Toccata." I had heard it for the first time when I was a sophomore in high school, clad in a dark green robe and yellow satin stole as a member of the Pilgrim Choir at First Congregational Church in Billings. Our organist, Mrs. Lawson, had played the dazzling piece requiring incredible skill and dexterity at the end of each of the three worship services we participated in on Easter Sunday. In my mind, the "Toccata" became so intertwined with that day that even years later, Easter wasn't Easter unless I could listen to the piece, on a recording, if not in a church.

A rush of excitement coursed through me as the first bright staccato notes—syncopated chords balanced by arpeggios—reverberated in the majestic space, moving by steps from high to low and back again. The notes in the sequence gradually moved lower, to be joined by the counterpoint of the slower, mellower bass. I felt a catch in my throat and started to weep. Leon, hearing me sniffle, turned to me, startled. "What's wrong?" he whispered.

"The music is so beautiful," I whispered back. The treble, dancing in the background, eventually reasserted itself over the bass, and the mood grew softer, calmer, with variations on the original theme. Later, after a clarion call of two pairs of notes, one low and one high, and a trio of the same notes—low-high-low—the opening theme came blazing back. A series of runs racing higher and higher on the keyboard followed, culminating with an extended single note at the top, shimmering with tension. The piece ended with a cadence of four full-bodied chords, the second higher than the first and held for an extra beat, and the last two repeating the first in quick succession.

Beautiful music never fails to move me. But that night, I was responding to more than the well-executed performance of a piece of music I cherished. In the magnificent setting of the Basilica, the "Toccata," with music's ability to span language and time and place and culture, wove together the disparate parts of me—the refugee child, the American adult, the middle-aged seeker of my Hungarian heritage—into a cohesive whole.

chapter twenty-two

On Behalf of My Father

DURING A PHONE call before we left for Hungary, my father made an unusual request. Learning the details of our earlier trip had apparently reminded him of a lost possession he hadn't thought about in a long time.

After our 2006 trip, I spent more time than usual in Billings. My mother broke her hip a couple of months after we got home. In the midst of her recovery, my father had an episode of intestinal bleeding that landed him in the ICU. I moved in with them for two months and became their caregiver. Dealing with their extensive needs left no time to talk with them about Leon's and my experiences in Hungary, to compare what we had seen with their memories. I had sent them an album of photos from our trip, but we never had an opportunity to go through it together. My first opening came only during a visit in August 2007, after my parents had both miraculously regained their health. One morning, my father and I lingered over breakfast at opposite ends of the mahogany dining room table, in the same spots we had occupied when I lived at home. Sunlight streamed through sheer curtains onto the fruit-patterned tablecloth covered with the *Billings Gazette*, the *Andrew Swanfeldt Crossword*

Puzzle Dictionary, a recent issue of *Harper's*, my mother's scribbled grocery list, a wire basket crammed with bottles of their vitamins and prescription medications. My mother was away running errands.

"Would you like to look at our Hungary pictures with me?" I asked my father. I was eager both to talk about what we had seen and to hear his thoughts about places he recognized.

"Of course," he answered, smiling. My father rarely shed his characteristic reserve, even with me, but he always seemed eager to spend time together if I suggested it.

Unfolding himself slowly from his chair, he leaned on his walker draped with multicolored Buddhist prayer flags, an expression of his lifelong interest in Eastern philosophies. I sat down in the middle of the sofa as he shuffled to the living room, his arthritic knees threatening to buckle with every step. He sank down on the far end, his long legs bent awkwardly in the space next to the coffee table. We balanced the album covered in burgundy vinyl on our laps. My father's blue eyes, only slightly dimmed behind their wire-rimmed glasses, studied with interest the photographs of Budapest as I pointed them out.

"There's me standing by the funicular," I said. "It was fun riding up to Castle Hill in a car that looked it was part of a kid's train set and watching the view of the Danube and the city unfold before us."

"I can imagine," my father said.

I led him on a tour of Castle Hill via photographs of immaculate Baroque buildings lining tidy streets, the asymmetrical spires of the Matthias Church and its ornate interior, the Fisherman's Bastion with its many turrets and expansive views of the city, and the massive, verdigris-domed Royal Palace.

"It looks like a beautiful area," he said.

"It is. They take really good care of it because lots of tourists go there."

As my father and I turned the pages of the album, our roles were reversed. After his letter that had set my quest in motion, I asked him questions and he answered them as best he could remember. Now, he was asking me questions and I was answering them. "Is that Margit Sziget (Margaret Island)?" he asked when we reached photographs of green spaces filled with trees and flowers.

"Yes," I answered, and then showed him pictures of the ruins of a thirteenth-century Dominican church and convent and a statue of Franz Liszt also located in the park.

"You saw a lot more of Hungary than we ever did," he chuckled. My father had few memories of his childhood and honeymoon trips to Budapest, and his unsuccessful job search there after the factory takeover had left little time for sightseeing.

"Here we are with Magdi at the restaurant where she and the violinist from the Gypsy band sang "Itt Hagyom a Falutokat" (I'm Leaving Your Village), I said. "She loved the story about your singing it in front of the ÁVO officer the night before you and Judy escaped."

"I can't believe I did that," my father said. "Your mother was sure he would arrest us."

"You were really brave," I said, touching his arm.

"I guess so," he answered, his eyes lowered, bashful.

At the scenes of Szombathely, he smiled in recognition at familiar landmarks: the railroad station, the main square, the

Lutheran church where he and my mother had been married and I was baptized. Farther on were photographs of our former home and the buildings that had been the original location of the Reich Gépgyár. "It looks really different," my father said, a wistful look on his face. No doubt he found it painful to see his former home stripped of its splendor, the buildings where he had spent so much of his younger life transformed for other uses. "The original smokestack!" he exclaimed with pleasure as we perused photographs of buildings a couple of blocks away that had housed the iron foundry where he had once supervised a hundred employees.

"The area is still called *öntöde* (foundry)," I told him, pointing out signs over the former main gate and next to a parking lot.

"At least they recognize what it once was," my father said. "That's something."

We turned to photographs of Marinka, the widow of his friend Sónyi. "What do you think about Sónyi's ending up with your old job?" I asked, referring to the revelatory newspaper article from the Szombathely library that I had sent him. When I first read it, I had worried about showing it to my father and revealing what to me seemed his friend's treachery. But I finally decided that he should be able to make up his own mind about his friend's motives. "Do you think he conspired with the Communists against you and Opapa?"

"I hate to think so," he said. My father, loyal and ethical in his dealings, no doubt found it inconceivable that a lifelong friend he helped had failed to adhere to that same code of conduct. It remained for me, more cynical than my father, to view Sónyi as the traitor he likely was.

More photos—of Vasvár; of Pinkafeld and the graveyard where Omama, Aunt Marianne and Uncle Zénó are buried; of Rohrbach, where we had lived. My father studied them with interest but demonstrated none of my mother's nostalgia for Austria. It was obvious his heart remained in Szombathely.

When he heard we were planning to return to Hungary in 2010, he told me what he most wanted from our hometown. "I'd like you to try to get a copy of my *oklevél*," he told me.

"What's that?" I asked.

"My mechanical engineering degree," he said. He had earned it at the Ingenieurschule Weimar in Germany in the early 1930s. That document, like most of our other possessions, had been left behind when we escaped. "Put an ad in the Szombathely paper and offer a reward to anyone who can give it to you," he instructed.

"I don't know, Dad; it seems like a waste of money," I said. After eight decades that had seen World War II and forty years of Communism, it seemed impossible that the document would have survived intact. And even if it had, why would anyone in town have kept it?

"Please try," he pleaded. Looking back over the twists and turns of his long life, my father must have longed to once again hold in his hands that concrete evidence of his achievement during a time when his future seemed limitless.

"Okay, I'll do it," I promised. Just as I had been unable to refuse him when he asked me to intercede with my mother during their arguments when I was a child, I couldn't refuse him now. My father would never return to Hungary. The least I could do was to act on his behalf in a matter that was clearly of paramount importance to him.

* * *

The day after the concert in the Basilica in Budapest, Leon and I were back in Szombathely. Our train pulled into the station on a Saturday, by coincidence, the day of the week that is the city's namesake and the day of the week that I was born there. Riding in a cab through now-familiar streets, arriving at the Hotel Wagner, settling into the same guest room overlooking Kossuth Lajos Street where we had stayed before, felt like putting on a pair of comfortable, well-worn slippers; like coming home.

First thing Monday morning, I walked to the main-square office of *Vas Népe,* the local newspaper I had combed for news of my birthplace online in the years between our trips. "Egy hirdetést szeretnék tenni az ujságba" (I'd like to place an ad in the paper), I told the woman at the desk. "My father is trying to locate a document from the 1930s." I handed her the ad copy I had typed in Hungarian to minimize the possibility of errors. Translated, it said: "A reward is offered to anyone who can produce the *oklevél* of Reich Sándor. Please contact Erika Reich Giles at the Hotel Wagner."

The woman studied the copy. "What an odd request," she said, frowning. "It doesn't really fit any of our ad categories."

"Do you have a miscellaneous category for ads that don't fit anywhere else?"

"Yes. I suppose we could put it there."

"Please run it for the next four days, while I'm still in town, so I can talk with anyone who comes forward," I said, trying to ignore the skepticism in the woman's eyes. She quoted me the price of the ad. Counting out the forints in payment, I was astonished by how much my skills conducting business in Hungarian had improved since 2006.

My father also asked me to try to find factory-related documents at the *levéltár* (document library), Szombathely's archives. He hadn't mentioned the facility to me before our previous trip, but seeing the materials I had sent him from the main library had no doubt whetted his appetite for more. The plain two-story concrete building was located on a small square opposite the entrance of our hotel, and Leon and I went there a couple of days after I placed the ad. With none of the hesitation I had felt at the library four years earlier, I strode to the front desk ahead of Leon.

"Do you have any documents related to the former Reich Gépgyár?" I asked the male receptionist in Hungarian.

"Please wait," he said, and picked up the receiver of a phone on the counter to make a call. Several people sat on folding chairs in the spare, tile-floored room that reeked of cigarette smoke.

Soon a wiry man wearing a smock appeared. "I'd be happy to talk with you about what you're looking for," he told me in Hungarian, leading us to a smoke-free side room. "Why are you interested in the documents?"

"I'm Gusztáv Reich's granddaughter," I said, feeling as proud as when I had identified myself to Mr. Horváth at our former home. "We're here for just a few days from the United States and I would like the documents for his son, my ninety-eight-year-old father."

"A relative of the owner!" the man exclaimed, beaming at me. "We'll get on it right away." He made a couple of calls, and soon a middle-aged man and woman arrived to help.

"We have many files relating to the factory," the man told me. "We'll try to find some that contain documents that might interest you."

As they left the room, I turned to the first man. "When we were here in 2006, I hesitated to ask for Reich Gépgyár documents at the main library," I said. "I wasn't sure how they would react." The man's positive reaction to the news that I was the owner's granddaughter made me more trusting than I had been at the library.

"Under Communism, such requests would have been frowned upon, but now, there is a renewed interest in history and private enterprise," he replied. "We do all we can to help."

The man and woman returned with three files. I flipped rapidly through the first two, filled with photographs of machinery from the failed Pohl factory that Opapa had bought to expand his own operation.

The last file contained the more personal information I sought. An unsigned letter dated May 1931 verified the purchase of the Pohl property by the Reich Gépgyár. A document dated January 31, 1935, detailed the taxable value of the real estate owned by my grandparents: their residence, the house where we had also lived, and the property housing the factory. The valuation was 258,350 pengő, which I later calculated was approximately $50,000 in 1935 US dollars, the equivalent of more than $900,000 in current dollars. A letter dated February 18, 1939, from my grandfather to the head of the Hungarian National Bank requested assurance that, as previously, they would facilitate the transfer of funds to the factory from a customer in Bulgaria to whom a shipment of machinery was being prepared. Opapa had signed the letter in his bold, slanted hand, "Gusztáv." Also in the file were a letter dated May 15, 1939, to my father about the return of a mechanical drawing he had requested, and a bookkeeping note in his handwriting.

Handling documents that my father and grandfather had held seventy years earlier, I could suddenly empathize with my father's desire for his *oklevél.* Concrete objects related to past events convey a meaning, an immediacy, that memories and spoken words alone cannot. Those frayed, yellowing sheets of paper made my father's and grandfather's day-to-day activities at the factory come alive to me in a way they never had before. And it moved me that, even though the factory was seized by the Communists, some unknown persons had valued those activities enough to preserve the evidence that they had occurred. The history of the Reich Gépgyár—my father's and grandfather's history—was not lost.

Leon and I spent several more days in Szombathely. We toured the *Romkert* (Garden of Ruins) that we had missed on our previous trip, an area filled with remnants of the Roman settlement of Savaria dating back to the first through fourth centuries—parts of roads and building walls and remarkably intact mosaics of geometric designs and plants. Located next to the *Székesegyház*, the main Catholic church, the *Romkert* is the scene of reenactments of Roman life during a festival held in the city every summer. In the suburb of Kámon north of the city, we strolled on winding walkways in a peaceful arboretum of evergreens and deciduous trees and rhododendrons that reminded us of home.

We also did more mundane things, like shop for snacks at the Spar grocery store. I selected a bunch of bananas in the produce department, but we couldn't figure out how to generate the slip of paper with the weight and cost that we knew from last time would be required at checkout. "I heard you speaking English and thought you might need help," a man standing nearby said to me in Hungarian. He showed us how to find the proper code for bananas and punch it into the machine.

"Köszönöm" (thank you), we both told him. Leon had picked up that Hungarian word as essential in 2006. The man's kindness touched us even more than that of the helpful staff at the *levéltár*, since he was a fellow shopper, rather than someone acting in an official capacity. If we asked, people were always willing to help, but otherwise, most people we encountered seemed reluctant even to make eye contact, much less speak. If we smiled at them, most did not smile back. My mother had told us such wariness was a legacy of the Communist era, when people didn't know whom they could trust. I probably hadn't noticed it as much in 2006 because of my single-minded focus on my quest.

No one responded to the ad about my father's *oklevél*. I wasn't surprised, but I felt disappointed on my father's behalf. I consoled myself with my success in obtaining the documents at the *levéltár*. It seemed fitting that I was able to fulfill my father's requests for information in libraries, since it was he who had introduced me to my first library when I was six years old.

I hadn't spoken to my father about revisiting Opapa's grave but knew he would approve. This time, undeterred by Marinka, Leon and I decorated his crypt with flowers twice. We visited once at the beginning of our stay, and once to say farewell at the end. The first bouquet was cluster of white lilies, red roses, and burgundy and white chrysanthemums and greenery that we attached to the headstone with a narrow ribbon to keep them from blowing away. On our second visit, we took red and white carnations set in a heavy glass vase. The concrete supporting the headstone was more chipped and worn than it had been in 2006, but I was pleased that our flowers brightened up the drab surface. Finally, I was honoring Opapa in the way I had wanted to do all along. A few days later in Pinkafeld, I would do the same with Aunt Marianne, Uncle Zénó, and Omama, adding to my growing sense of peace and closure.

At home, I visited cemeteries only occasionally—in Seattle on Memorial Day to honor Slim and Saimie, friends a generation older who'd acted as surrogate parents during the early years of our marriage; in Billings once or twice a year to place flowers on the graves of my brother Robie and my Nagymama and Nagypapa. But through our visits to Opapa's grave, I began to grasp the appeal of tending graves on a more frequent basis, not only as a gesture of love and respect, but also as a way to feel connected to those whose remains inhabit them. If I lived in Szombathely, I would revisit the cemetery from time to time, joining the elderly people, mostly women in skirts and cardigans, trudging along the paths carrying bouquets and clippers on Sunday afternoons. I would commune with my grandfather in death as I had never been able to do in life. I would reflect on the Reich Gépgyár that he and my father had worked so hard to build. I would imagine that the devastating loss of the factory hadn't happened—that I had known the love of my grandfather and been loved by a father able to live out his hopes and dreams.

chapter twenty-three

Letting Go

YET AGAIN, LEON and I stood among graves in a cemetery. The sun shimmered in the cloudless blue September sky and the air was still, with no trace of the wind that had gusted around us when we had visited this hilltop expanse in my mother's hometown of Vasvár in 2006. Then, we had been here at her request, searching without success for the grave of her family's landlord. Now, we were here because Erzsi wanted to pay her respects at her parents' grave before we had lunch at the home of her daughter, Andi, who had later found the right grave for us. We hung back a respectful distance as Erzsi placed a bouquet of white chrysanthemums in the vase next to the charcoal-gray headstone. She then moved to the foot of the crypt, its planter overflowing with ivy and juniper, and bowed her head. The warm air made me drowsy, and I daydreamed about meeting János, Judy's birth father, on a subsequent visit to town. This time, my sister Judy had asked me to do whatever was necessary to make contact with him, even if it meant walking up to his house and knocking on the door. In her late sixties, she apparently realized that her window of opportunity for learning more about him than he had revealed during their correspondence years earlier was rapidly shrinking. And I remained as curious about him as ever.

My eyes drifted from Erzsi to the surrounding graves. Two rows ahead of where we stood, I noticed an imposing headstone of the same dark granite as her parents' marker, but its sides were curved, rather than straight. The crypt beneath it was at least twice as wide. I stared at the name and dates on the stone, carved in plain letters under a large cross. Only after a few seconds did they register: Oroszlán János, 1922–2009. Judy's birth father. There could be no mistake. My mother was born in 1923, and I knew she and her former husband had been close in age. "János died and that's his grave over there," I whispered to Leon. Given our fruitless search in the cemetery four years earlier, we could hardly believe that I had located the grave without even trying.

Coupled with my amazement was a sharp, unexpected sense of loss. I was too late. Never would I meet or even see this man who was a significant part of our family, even in his absence. Never would I be able to describe to Judy how a tilt of his head, a facial expression, an inflection in his voice, reminded me of her, nor would I fulfill my secret hope that I could help them reconcile. Never would my mother's former spouse shed light on the woman my mother had been when they were together.

It was possible Erzsi knew that János was Judy's father. She could have learned that fact from Uncle Laci during one of his visits to Hungary, or from Aunt Évi, who corresponded with her on a regular basis. But if she didn't know and I told her, word might get back to my mother through my aunt. Unwilling to risk upsetting my mother, I said nothing to Erzsi about my startling discovery. We left the cemetery and drove to Andi's house. We had a pleasant visit with her and her husband, Józsi, over a tasty lunch of chicken *paprikás* she had prepared for us. Afterward, they led us on a walking tour of Vasvár. One of our first stops was my mother's former home. Next to the double doors leading to the house and the backyard was a marble plaque that hadn't been there last time. Dated 2010, it announced that Dr. Amália Regész Mozsolics, a prominent historical researcher, had been born in the house one hundred years earlier. She was the daughter of Amália Feszta Mozsolics, Nagymama and Nagypapa's former landlord, whose grave Leon and I had searched for in vain in 2006. It was interesting to see the bronze likeness of the woman Leon and I had mistakenly honored on behalf of Aunt Évi and my mother. At the same time, I couldn't help thinking of other former inhabitants of the house, my mother and her family among them, who had contributed to the life of the town but would remain invisible and unsung.

We sauntered westward down the street. "My mother and Aunt Évi went to a convent school," I told my companions. "I thought it had been in the building next to the church on the main square, but my mother said no. Do you know where it was?"

"Right here," Józsi answered as we came to a wide, coral-colored, two-story building topped by a cross just a few doors from their house.

The building, now converted to apartments, had housed the school where my mother had been forced to spend an extra year solely to watch over her younger sister. Massive blue doors led to a verdant courtyard where they no doubt played at recess with their friends on nice days. From the building's many windows, especially those on the second floor, they would have had views of the town below. I liked that, rather than attending school in the dark, low-ceilinged spaces where I had earlier imagined my mother, she had spent her schooldays in this lighter, airier place, a counterbalance to the darkness that came later.

Back in our hotel room in Szombathely that night, I called Judy. "János died in 2009," I said, explaining our serendipitous discovery of his grave.

"What a coincidence that he's buried right by where you were with Erzsi," she said. "Thanks for letting me know." True to her nature, she gave no sign of shock or distress, but she did ask me to put flowers on his grave. She also passed the news on to our mother. If she hoped the information would persuade her to start talking about János, she was wrong. Our mother was as reticent as ever, hinting only that there was little good to say about her former spouse.

* * *

A stark contrast to her attitude toward her current spouse, my father. Her love for him was especially evident as he recovered from his bleeding episode in 2007. A couple of days after my mother called to tell me what happened, I flew home to Billings. She met me at the airport. She looked small and frail and vulnerable as she hobbled toward me with a cane, still recovering from her broken hip. "Thank you for coming," she said.

"I wouldn't dream of being anywhere else," I said, hugging her.

"I'm really worried about your father," she said, her eyes brimming with tears.

"So am I. But let's wait to see what the tests show," I said, even as I tried to quiet my own fears that the colon cancer diagnosed several years earlier had recurred.

In the ICU at St. Vincent Medical Center, my father lay on a bed in one of several recessed spaces encircling a nurses' station. He looked more robust, less ashen than I had feared, given his extensive blood loss, but he slept much of the time. My mother and I kept vigil on either side of his bed, too distracted to do more than watch him, talk to him when he awakened, and murmur desultory comments to each other. Sometimes, she smoothed his hair or touched his cheek. Tubes for liquids and medication snaked into his arm and a monitor for vital signs beeped overhead. When the greenish squiggles of his heartbeat moving across the screen seemed more irregular than usual or his blood pressure dropped to levels that seemed too low, we exchanged anxious glances. More detailed conversations took place over soup and sandwiches in the hospital cafeteria.

"I don't want him to have the colonoscopy," she said. "I'm not sure I want to know that the cancer has come back."

"It could also show that it hasn't," I pointed out.

"What if they sedate him and he doesn't wake up?"

"He will," I said, probably to convince myself as much as her.

"If he's going to die, I want him at home with me, not in this place," she said, dissolving into tears.

"Oh, Mom, don't go there," I said, reaching for her hand, more contorted than ever from her rheumatoid arthritis. "Not when we don't know what's going to happen."

"I can't help it … I don't want to lose him."

"I know. I don't, either."

In the end, my father had the test and it showed no signs of cancer. His doctors told us he had experienced spontaneous bleeding from diverticula in his intestine, not uncommon among the elderly, exacerbated by a blood thinner he had been taking.

My mother and I went out to dinner that night to celebrate. We toasted to my father's health with white wine, surrounded by Tiffany glass and antiques at George Henry's, a special occasion restaurant in Billings. As we waited for our entrées, my mother grew pensive. "Nagymama and I never got along," she suddenly blurted.

"You didn't?" I'd heard innuendos, from Judy and possibly even from her, but never had she spoken so directly to me about her relationship with her mother.

She studied her wineglass. "No, and I never could understand why," she added ruefully.

"It's ironic that she and I were so close when I was growing up," I said.

"Yes, she really cared about you. It's probably different between grandmothers and their granddaughters."

"I sometimes feel like my relationship with you is like yours was with her," I ventured, hesitant to say too much, but also wanting to take advantage of this unexpected opening.

"Maybe ... You weren't an easy child to raise."

"I know," I said with an embarrassed smile.

"You didn't do what you were told. You argued."

"I have a mind of my own, just like you do," I said. I recalled how I hadn't wanted to stay at home with my brother Robie the day he ran away from home, or go with my parents and Judy the day we witnessed the murder. In those cases, my parents might have done well to let me have my way. But most of the time, I took the opposing view because being obstinate seemed to be in my genes.

She sighed. "We *are* a lot alike."

"We sure are. Look how emotional we both get."

"Did I ever tell you that when you were a baby, my breast milk didn't have all the nutrition you needed?"

"Yes, you mentioned it. It must have been hard to cope with a baby who wouldn't stop crying even after you fed her."

"It turned out okay. The doctor gave me some medicine, and soon my milk was fine," she said.

"But I wonder if there was some lasting effect," I said. Had some aspect of maternal-infant bonding failed to take place at a critical time? I suspected it had. A more solid foundation might have made our relationship less fragile, less prone to deteriorate into clashes that could be difficult to resolve.

"No," my mother said. The firm set of her lips told me we had gone as far as she would go. I was grateful that she had been willing to open up as much as she had and didn't press her. We spent the rest the evening discussing the events of the past few days, warmed by our relief about my father. Our sense of shared intimacy also lingered.

From the ICU, my father was transferred to a regular hospital room, and later to a rehabilitation unit to build up his strength enough that he could return home. I supported my mother as she enticed him with food to help him gain weight, encouraged him during physical therapy sessions complicated by his unsteady knees, accompanied him on longer and longer walks in the hallways. Her devotion to my father permeated those long days at the hospital, as did the force of her will that left no room for the possibility that her husband of sixty years would leave her. And he didn't.

My mother and I connected most closely in the midst of crises—sitting in her darkened bedroom, crying together after Nagypapa's funeral; sharing our grief on the phone after Robie died; comforting each other when my father was in the ICU and his life hung in the balance. Perhaps it's because our earliest connections occurred amid the crises of my mother giving birth to me in the aftermath of the factory takeover, of her carrying me in her arms during her perilous escape from our homeland. It's said that crisis creates opportunity. Perhaps my mother and I needed those darker moments from time to time to remind us of what we meant to each other.

* * *

Back in Vasvár a couple of days after my phone call with Judy, I bought a bouquet of red roses, white chrysanthemums, and greenery tied with a ribbon inscribed with her name and "Emlékszem" (I Remember). I placed it in the vase next to János's headstone. I thought not only about him and Judy, but also about him and my mother. Whatever there had been between them so many years ago, it was clear that my father was the only husband she cared about. No doubt it was her fierce loyalty to him that prevented her from revealing the existence of János to Judy and me, that kept her from talking about him even after we knew. I might not have handled the situation the way she did, but the hours I spent in Vasvár, seeing where she had grown from a child into a young woman, walking the streets where she had walked, underscored for me just how different her life had been from mine. How could I judge her? What I *could* do, though, was to let go of János and my need to know more about him, once and for all.

chapter twenty-four

Onward

FROM VASVÁR, LEON and I drove fifty miles southeast to Lake Balaton. We had hoped on our previous trip to visit this popular vacation spot that my parents had talked about but ran out of time. The lake, fifty miles long and eight miles wide, is the largest body of fresh water in central Europe, providing landlocked Hungary with the closest thing to a seashore. On a rise at the junction of Route 84 and the road ringing the lake, Route 71, we caught our first glimpse of its blue waters, source of the *süllő*, the perch we had eaten at the fish restaurant in Budapest in 2006. That flavorful fish would forever be linked in my mind with the night the Gypsy band played "I'm Leaving Your Village" and Magdi sang along, as my father had done fifty-eight years earlier.

We headed west to explore the coastline and passed a sign for Balatongyörök, the hamlet where Omama had lived with Aunt Marianne and her family after the Communists forced her from her home in the wake of Opapa's death. On the far side of the road from the lake, stucco houses, year-round residences and summer homes, dotted the green but mostly treeless hillside. I had anticipated driving on a road that hugged the shoreline, but the lake was in fact several blocks away, giving us only occasional glimpses of sun glinting on the waves. Farther on, billboards and pizza joints and campgrounds and various amusements appeared. "Ugh," I said. The honky-tonk atmosphere dispelled any visions I'd had of communing with nature.

"This isn't quite what I expected," Leon agreed. We decided to turn around and explore the town where my grandmother and other relatives had lived in one room of a villa the Communists had appropriated from Omama's brother-in-law, Kálmán, though I didn't know where the house was located.

We turned from the main road onto a charming main street that sloped toward the lake. Lining it were tidy houses; some, with thatched roofs, dated back to the 1800s. On a pedestal in an open space was a bust of Kossuth Lajos, the oft-honored hero of Hungary's failed 1848 Revolution against Austria. Across the street was a small whitewashed church. I imagined Omama strolling here, each step leaden with grief at losing not only her beloved husband of thirty-seven years, but also the home where they had raised Aunt Marianne and my father. At the foot of the incline, train tracks separated the street from a park shaded by deciduous trees. There, a limestone monolith ringed by red and white flowers commemorated fallen soldiers from World War I.

Beyond the park was the lake. A jetty of large rocks with a sidewalk down the middle beckoned us. We walked out to the end, passing several fishermen casting their lines from the rocks, perhaps trying to catch *süllő*. With water surrounding us on three sides, it felt as though we were on a boat as we studied the south shore, indistinct in midday haze. To the east were the prominent hills of Badacsony, where the grapes for the *szürkebarát*, the pinot gris we had enjoyed on our first night in Budapest in 2006, were grown. The water appeared greenish up close, its surface ruffled by a fresh breeze. Yet no boats with billowing sails skimmed over the waves. Back on shore, we watched a white swan and two brown cygnets in a cove, diving with long necks under the surface of the water in search of food before gliding away.

At a smoky souvenir shop across from the railroad station, we selected postcards to send to my parents and to keep as mementos of Omama's former home. Afterward, we found a waterfront restaurant down the shoreline from the park. We sat at a table shaded by an umbrella from the bright sun and feasted on *lángos,* Hungary's version of Native American fry bread, flattish pieces of fried dough the size of a small pizza. As my family had done when I was a child, we smeared them with cloves of raw garlic for added flavor. They weren't quite like the *lángos* my mother and Nagymama and Aunt Évi had made; theirs were smaller and less dense. Still, eating the delicacy reminded me how excited Suzie and I had always been when it was on the menu. Preparing the dough, cutting it into pieces, covering it with a cloth, waiting for it to rise, and frying each individual piece required more time than my mother and grandmother and aunt often had to spare, making *lángos* a rare treat.

That afternoon, looking out at Lake Balaton, tastes from my childhood lingering on my tongue, I felt a surge of joy—at the warmth of the sun, at the sloshing of the waves on the shore, at the breeze blowing in my hair, at being back in Hungary with Leon. During both trips, I had searched for and connected with a past I had known only through the memories of others. I had felt, as never before, the heartbreak of my family's losses. But rather than hold me back, those discoveries set me free to create my own memories in Hungary, to enjoy my homeland for its own sake. The water stretching in all directions offered broader vistas than those we had seen elsewhere in the country, suggesting limitless possibilities, an expansion of my own vision of what my homeland would mean to me in the future.

On the way back to Szombathely, we decided to stop in Sümeg, a town defined by a steep basalt hill jutting up from the countryside with a thirteenth-century castle on its summit. We found our way from a town center filled with picturesque Baroque buildings shaded from the late-afternoon sun by trees turning red and gold to a cobblestoned pathway winding up the hill. We parked our car and joined other visitors climbing upward. Fifteen minutes later, we were at the gates of a fortress that had enabled the Hungarians to hold off the Turks in the mid-1500s. Now the structure, its walls still intact, is a tourist attraction, complete with displays of medieval jousting. There was no performance that day, but we did see costumed horsemen practicing in a riding facility in the town far below. I photographed Leon with his head in stocks once used for prisoners, and we gaped at the cannons and giant cannonballs that had thwarted enemies. We climbed wooden stairs to reach the battlements and were treated to a view even more expansive than that at Lake Balaton. Western Hungary spread below us—the red roofs of the town; low mountains to the south; rolling hills; farmland bordered by trees; the horizon, bluish in the distance. From this vantage point, the vastness of the landscape with the cloudless blue sky overhead mirrored the wide reaches of Montana from my childhood, narrowing the gap between the ambivalent child I had been and the middle-aged woman standing on a firmer foundation.

Another day, we again retraced the route of our escape. We took the Nárai Road from Szombathely as we had done four years earlier, but this time the weather was sunny and mild, closer to the actual conditions on those two days in June 1948. There were more oaks, beeches, and elms than I remembered. Trees lining the road past Szombathely's suburbs, large stands of trees acting as windbreaks between harvested fields, thick forests of trees. The town of Nárai seemed more cosmopolitan than before, with even a tattoo parlor, and a large industrial area on the far side of the town. And near the border, Pornóapáti seemed larger and less forbidding, with people chatting in yards and strolling on the street. Some stared at us, curious, as I took photographs.

Was my memory faulty? Or had these places actually changed in the four years since we had last been here? No doubt it was a combination of both. Given the gaps in my own memory after such a short period of time, I realized how remarkable it was that my mother and father had remembered *any* details about experiences that had occurred in the midst of a major upheaval in their lives more than half a century earlier. Small wonder that even those they did remember didn't necessarily coincide with each other. And if these places I was seeing had indeed changed since I last saw them, what about the changes since my parents' time, through forty years of Communism and its aftermath? The Hungary I was seeing was likely only a faint imprint of their Hungary. As much as I had learned, I could never fully recapture their lives here.

This trip, my parents and I didn't exchange lengthy phone

calls as we had before. Since I had done so once, I felt no need to try to give them a vicarious experience of traveling in our homeland. At the same time, aware of our previous discoveries, my parents—and especially my mother—seemed to feel no need to influence what we saw or did, or to guard against our stumbling upon old secrets. Perhaps they sensed that, more and more, I was seeing and experiencing *my* Hungary, not theirs.

Beyond Pornóapáti, Leon and I drove past the former convent or monastery, to the spot where, in 2006, the road had ended at a gate-arm barrier and amid a thick tangle of shrubs, and an Austrian guard had studied us through binoculars. This time, the road passed a small building that might once have been a guardhouse and continued unimpeded into Austria. "What's going on?" I asked Leon.

"I don't know," he answered. "Maybe it has something to do with their not asking to see our passports when we arrived at the airport in Budapest." The omission had seemed odd, but we didn't dwell on it at the time. I was only too happy to avoid my previous experience of handing over my passport to a stone-faced passport officer who stared at it far longer than he did Leon's, wondering whether he would detain me because I was born in Hungary.

* * *

Near the end of our 2006 trip, I'd had another scare involving my passport. Leon and I were shopping on the second floor of the cavernous Central Market in Budapest, browsing for gifts in stalls filled with embroidered tablecloths and ceramic vases decorated with colorful floral designs and T-shirts and purses imprinted with symbols of the city. I selected a table runner for my niece and reached into the security pouch hanging on the inside of my waistband for my credit card to pay for it. Pulling it out, I realized that my passport, which I also kept there, was missing.

"I don't have my passport," I told Leon.

"Are you sure?" he asked. "Maybe you put it somewhere else this morning."

With a rising sense of panic, I rummaged through the large purse I wore slung across my body to discourage would-be muggers, where I kept my wallet and our guidebooks. "It's not here, either."

"Maybe you left it at the hotel."

"Maybe … I don't know," I said, momentarily unable to think, to recall the steps I had taken to prepare for our shopping expedition.

"Do you want to buy the runner?"

"No, I'm done shopping. We need to find my passport," I said. "Sajnálom" (I'm sorry), I said to the disappointed saleswoman as I put my credit card away and handed the runner back to her.

We raced downstairs, past food stalls with hanging sausages and aromas of paprika, and out the main entrance. My heart pounded as we wove among the jostling crowds on Váci utca—past a Gypsy woman with tanned, wrinkled skin begging with dramatic hand gestures; past women selling tablecloths draped in front of their bodies like dresses; past carts loaded with postcards and key rings and other trinkets. I said little as I pondered the complex bureaucratic process that would no doubt be involved to replace my passport if it was lost or stolen, a process that could certainly not be completed in time for our departure the next morning.

"How are you doing?" Leon asked, taking my hand.

"So-so. I'd love to have an excuse to stay here longer, but changing our airplane tickets would cost a bundle."

"Let's not worry about that unless we need to," he said.

By the time we reached the Chain Bridge with its vistas of boats floating on the Danube, I felt calmer. The river's peaceful waters reminded me of Leon's frequent advice to "go with the flow" when I was upset rather than resisting the inevitable and making things harder for myself.

Back in our room, we sifted through brochures and guidebooks scattered on tables, but my passport wasn't among them. I unlocked the safe on a shelf in the closet. Nothing. "I guess it's gone," I said, scanning the room. Finally, I spotted a drawer in a table where I sometimes kept papers. I pulled it open. There, just where I left it, lay my passport. I was relieved. At the same time, I felt a twinge of disappointment that we would not be extending our stay in this homeland that was insinuating itself into my heart.

* * *

Now we were on a road leading to Austria with no apparent need for a passport. A strange sensation. To my surprise, I hesitated to follow it, even though I could finally have replicated the route my mother had likely taken when she escaped from Hungary with me in her arms. My parents' doubts, their legacy of distrust, dogged me still. I felt compelled to turn around and retrace the route we had taken before, northward along the border to Route 89, to the official border crossing near Nárda. There, we found two drab cinder-block Passport Control buildings, one in Hungary and the other a short distance away in Austria. No barrier stood between them. Their windows were dark, their doors shut. The area was deserted.

We later learned that in December 2007, more than a year after our last trip, Hungary had implemented the rules of the Schengen Agreement of 1985, which in 1999 was folded into the laws of the European Union. My homeland joined the other twenty-five countries of the eurozone that allowed travelers to move freely among them, without the use of passports.

Leon and I sat in our car near the two abandoned buildings. "I can't believe it," I said, shaking my head.

"It's pretty amazing," Leon said. "Remember when we saw the Iron Curtain in 1979?"

"Who could forget? And remember that guard who wouldn't let me take a picture at the border crossing at Klingenbach? What a huge change this is." I shifted my gaze between the dark green forest-covered foothills of the Alps in Austria and rolling hills of golden wheat stubble in Hungary, glad to be here in this place, at this time. I thought of how Hungary had progressed from borders where guards prevented people from leaving, requiring my family to be smuggled to freedom; to the barbed wire and minefields of the Iron Curtain that imprisoned its citizens for forty years; to normal border controls used by free countries; to no barriers at all. The changes reflected my own journey—a journey that had broken down the barriers between me and the heritage I had once tried to escape. I smiled at Leon. "Let's go," I said. Turning the key in the ignition, I pressed my foot on the gas and crossed that open border into the rest of my Hungarian-American life.

Epilogue

It's hard to reconcile the Hungary I last visited in 2010 with the country that in recent years has most often been mentioned in the international news as a vivid example of the right-wing nationalism sweeping much of the world. Viktor Orbán, who became the prime minister after his Fidesz Party won the national election that year, remains the country's leader as of the publication of this book. His strong authoritarian bent is reminiscent of other autocratic leaders in the country's history.

In 2015, Hungary was also in the news for erecting a fence to stop Syrian and other refugees from entering the country. It was understandable that a country as poor as Hungary had little to spare for desperate people who only wanted to pass through to countries like Germany that had more to offer them. But it was also ironic that, less than three decades after the fall of the Iron Curtain, a fence that had imprisoned its citizens, Hungary erected a fence to keep people out. I wanted my homeland to display more compassion toward people who were not unlike my family when we came to the United States as refugees.

I'm dismayed by such developments in Hungary, but no more so than by what happened in the United States during the Trump era, with its focus on border walls and immigration quotas and a turning away from cooperation with other countries, including our allies. No doubt, just like me and fellow left-leaning citizens, there are many in Hungary who don't agree with what their government is doing, but they have limited opportunities to effect change. I can't judge them. Like me, they probably do what they can and cling to the hope that things will eventually change for the better.

Regardless of what happens in Hungary in the future, it will forever be the place that enabled me to become whole. For that, I will always be grateful.

Acknowledgments

First, I would like to thank Priscilla Long, who sparked my love of writing essays and memoir in her personal essay class that was part of the Certificate Program in Nonfiction Writing at the University of Washington. She also helped me develop some of the essays that became part of this book. I am also grateful to Barbara Sjoholm, who guided me in finding a viable structure for the book and assisted with developmental editing. Thanks also to Brooke Warner, who assisted with copy editing, and Katya Fishman of Endeavorink and Amie Norris of Words Reworked, who also provided valuable assistance.

I greatly appreciate Laurie Minsk and Linda Oman, two members of my first writers group, who helped with early versions of essays that ended up in the book. Thanks also to Betty Ruddy, a later addition to that group, who also provided helpful input and encouragement in our one-on-one discussions and as a first reader of the book. I appreciate the members of my second writers group, who helped me further develop essays and provided input into the book itself: Lisa Weil, Judith Gille, David Bauman, John Ashford, and Mary Oak. Thanks also to my other first readers, Kay Crawford and Kathy Philip, for their valuable insights.

Most of all, I am grateful to my husband, Leon Giles, for his wholehearted encouragement and support throughout my writing career, and especially during the process of writing this book and getting it published. I couldn't have done it without him.

About the Author

Erika Reich Giles spent her social work career helping children move out of the foster care system by facilitating their return to their birth parents or placing them for adoption. She began writing essays and memoir after she remembered a traumatic incident from her childhood, not unlike those experienced by some of her clients. Her work gave her an understanding of family dynamics and the effects of trauma that helped her unravel her own past for this book. Her essays have been published in *The Seattle Times*, *Crab Orchard Review*, *Clackamas Literary Review*, *North Dakota Quarterly*, *Ascent*, *Under the Sun*, *Clockhouse Review*, *Tahoma Literary Review*, and in two anthologies.

Erika's own refugee background has made her passionate about helping immigrants and refugees learn English. She has led conversation groups for English learners for more than a decade, believing that the more people connect with the language of the country they live in, the more likely they will be to acclimate and achieve their full potential there. Seattle-area residents for more than forty years, she and her husband now live in Portland, Oregon.

Organizations, groups, and individuals who are interested in exploring any of the topics in *Becoming Hungarian* and/or conversation groups for people learning English can contact Erika through www.erikagiles.com or at erikagiles@comcast.net.

www.ingramcontent.com/pod-product-compliance
Lightning Source LLC
LaVergne TN
LVHW100519110826
845146LV00002B/700

* 9 7 9 8 2 1 8 3 3 6 9 7 4 *